Praise For *The Traveler's Path*

"We travel. But why? What kinds of journeys are driven more by purpose than by pleasure? And how does an outward journey impact the inward journey of our souls? What is the root of our restlessness, and where might it lead? Douglas Brouwer turns to illuminating questions like these to look at all our experiences of travel—exploratory vacations, pilgrimages, mission trips, and more—through a reflective, spiritual lens. Partly memoir, these pages are also infused with the secular and sacred wisdom of others. What shines through are the experiences of this well-traveled pastor that have transformed his life and will enrich any reader who sets off on a journey."

Wesley Granberg-Michaelson, General Secretary Emeritus of the Reformed Church in America and the author of *Without Oars: Casting Off into a Life of Pilgrimage*

"In a true journey of the soul, Douglas Brouwer paints an exquisite portrait that echoes my own experience of leading pilgrimages to the Holy Land—not as a mere journey across continents, but as a profound voyage of spirit. From the sacred stones of the Holy Land to the remote corners of the world, this book traces the footsteps of pilgrims past and present, each journey woven with faith, purpose, and a desire to seek both within and beyond. Through the lens of mission trips and sacred travels, Brouwer shows us that the act of pilgrimage is not only about the places we visit but the transformation that unfolds along the way. This is a book that will stir the soul, beckoning us to explore the deeper meanings of travel, to walk in the footsteps of the divine, and to serve with open hearts wherever we are called."

Rick Ricart, Founder and President of Imagine Tours & Travel

"This book is an adventure. Invited in by personal stories, this well-crafted book drew me to explore my own thoughts and experiences. That's because Douglas Brouwer's honest commentary on his growth allows others to look honestly at their process. I was very impressed by the amount of research into various views of travel, which added significantly to broadening my own understanding and provided a solid base for further discussions. There were two bits of writing that caught my attention. One was Doug's quote of Thomas Merton's words spoken close to the end of his life. In essence they were: We are all one but imagine that we are not. The other was a comment made about a self-discovery of his own. He came to understand that one of his gifts was being able to listen. I experienced this quality a few years ago when he listened, over long emails, to my own processing of finding the book I was wanting to write. His ability to hear my personal travel into that book allowed it to happen—a gift from a fellow traveler."

Judith E. Bowen, author of *The Mystical Symphony, A Memoir of Healing, Vision and Wonder*

"As researchers have documented, and as Douglas Brouwer has experienced, human experience in varied cultures expands people's perspectives, curiosity, creativity, and empathy. In this memoir of his own life travels—from family vacations to mission trips to pilgrimages to ministering in varied states and nations—he explores lessons learned. And he bids us to consider how we, too, by travels beyond our comfort zone, might grow in spiritual and cultural understanding."

David G. Myers, social psychologist and author of *How Do We Know Ourselves: Curiosities and Marvels of the Human Mind*

"In warm, wise, conversational prose, Douglas Brouwer reflects in these pages on a lifetime of rich and varied travel: vacations, pilgrimages, mission trips, job relocations, and more. He alerts us to the pitfalls of mere tourism, the fleeting seductions of consuming yet another exotic site. But he also shares the best that travel has to offer—lessons in humility, in learning how to listen and really see, in how to offer and—even more difficult!—accept hospitality. He is especially alert to the spiritual dimension in all these encounters. In meeting so many others, he shows, we may come to know ourselves better, and in roaming far afield, may finally recognize our true home. This is a wonderful guide both to going abroad and to searching deeper within."

James Bratt, Calvin College emeritus professor and scholar of American religious history

"Part travel memoir, part meditation on the meanings of our movements, this winsome and wise book invites us to thoughtful reflection on who we become through the journeys we take."

David I. Smith, Director, Kuyers Institute for Christian Teaching and Learning, Calvin University

The Traveler's Path

Finding Spiritual Growth and
Inspiration Through Travel

Douglas J. Brouwer

For more information and further discussion, visit

ReformedJournal.com

Copyright © 2025 by Douglas J. Brouwer

Scripture quotations are from the New Revised Standard Version Updated Edition. Copyright © 2021 National Council of Churches of Christ in the United States of America. Used by permission. All rights reserved worldwide.

ISBN: 978-1-64180-212-3

Version 1.0

Cover design by Rick Nease. RickNeaseArt.com

Cover photo by Mary R. Talen, PhD

Published by Reformed Journal Books
Publishing services by Front Edge Publishing
42807 Ford Road, No. 234
Canton, MI, 48187

Front Edge Publishing books are available for discount bulk purchases for events, corporate use and small groups. Special editions, including books with corporate logos, personalized covers and customized interiors are available for purchase. For more information, contact Front Edge Publishing at info@FrontEdgePublishing.com

Contents

Chapter 1.	Our Origin Story	1
Chapter 2.	The Gift of Curiosity	16
Chapter 3.	Does Travel Make Us Better People?	26
Chapter 4.	Making Room for Those Who Cannot Travel	37
Chapter 5.	A Protestant Passport to Pilgrimage	50
Chapter 6.	'Go Into All the World'	66
Chapter 7.	Daring to Get Lost	76
Chapter 8.	So Many Roads!	84
Chapter 9.	Is a Mission Trip a Pilgrimage?	98
Chapter 10.	Revisiting Babel	113
Chapter 11.	Reframing the Art of Travel	123
Chapter 12.	*Stolpersteine:* Stumbling Stones	136
Chapter 13.	There's No Place Like 'Home'	146
Chapter 14.	The Romance of 'Barbarous Coasts'	157
Chapter 15.	'You Can't Go Home Again'	165
Chapter 16.	How Can We Write the Final Chapter?	177
Acknowledgments		192

Contents

Chapter 1. Our Origin Story 1
Chapter 2. The Gift of Curiosity 16
Chapter 3. Does Travel Make Us Better People? 26
Chapter 4. Making Room for Those Who Cannot Travel . . 37
Chapter 5. A Protestant Passport to Pilgrimage 50
Chapter 6. 'Go Into All the World' 66
Chapter 7. Daring to Get Lost 76
Chapter 8. So Many Roads! 84
Chapter 9. Is a Mission Trip a Pilgrimage? 98
Chapter 10. Revisiting Babel 113
Chapter 11. Reframing the Art of Travel 123
Chapter 12. *Stolpersteine:* Stumbling Stones 136
Chapter 13. There's No Place Like 'Home' 146
Chapter 14. The Romance of 'Barbarous Coasts' 157
Chapter 15. 'You Can't Go Home Again' 165
Chapter 16. How Can We Write the Final Chapter? 177
Acknowledgments 192

I

Our Origin Story

*"In the beginning God created the heavens and the earth.
And the earth was without form, and void;
And darkness was upon the face of the deep.
And the Spirit of God moved upon the face of the waters."*
Genesis 1:1-2, KJV

Travel is our origin story.

Our travels—perhaps from or toward a home, either voluntarily or involuntarily—are experiences we share with people around the world. And yet, in decades of preaching and teaching, as well as listening to others preach and teach, I have not heard a satisfying exploration of this theme that runs throughout our faith traditions.

In the creation story shared by billions of Jews, Christians, and Muslims, God made the first move in fashioning the world. Genesis tells us: "God moved upon the face of the waters." Soon after, the first human beings, Adam and Eve, moved too—this time involuntarily. In Genesis 3, we read that "the Lord God sent them forth from the garden of Eden." Then, in the very next chapter, Adam and Eve's son Cain heads into exile (after murdering his brother, Abel) with the words: "I shall be a fugitive and a wanderer on the earth." And today, nearly 120 million people worldwide are among those "fugitives and wanderers"—refugees, asylum seekers, and others who have been "forcibly displaced" from their homes, about twice as many as a decade ago, according to the UN Refugee Agency.

Even the consensus of paleoanthropologists—the secular study of our human origins—is that *Homo sapiens* arose hundreds of thousands of years ago in Africa and migrated from there to the farthest corners of our planet.

So, travel is our origin story. With this book, I am challenging readers to discover the connections between our own "travel" within this larger movement of peoples—and the timeless call of God through our religious traditions—so we might glimpse the greater depth, breadth, and meaning of our collective movement, our setting out and going places.

Defining 'travel'

I didn't make up this expanded definition of travel. A global conversation has been unfolding for decades about how our movement in various forms can serve as a basis for a constructive conversation about what unites and what divides us. In fact, the 2024 consensus on the definition of "travel" as cooperatively edited by the thousands of editors of the Wikipedia encyclopedia is broader than most of us might guess:

> Travel is the movement of people between distant geographical locations. ... Reasons for traveling include recreation, holidays, rejuvenation, tourism or vacationing, research travel, the gathering of information, visiting people, volunteer travel for charity, migration to begin life somewhere else, religious pilgrimages and mission trips, business travel, trade, commuting, obtaining health care, waging or fleeing war, for the enjoyment of traveling, or other reasons. Travelers may use human-powered transport such

as walking or bicycling; or vehicles, such as public transport, automobiles, trains, ferries, boats, cruise ships, and airplanes.

As we try to define travel today, we discover that all this movement *defines us*.

Travel changes who we are as families, communities, nations, and even as a living species on Earth. It's that truth about the transformative power of travel that lies at the heart of the world's great religious traditions. It's a truth sometimes called the "monomyth" by followers of Joseph Campbell and Carl Jung who point out that—as much as we may love our homes—most religious origin stories are rooted in setting out on a journey. In Buddhism, for example, Campbell points out that Siddhartha Gautama was transformed when he set out on a quest to find the origins of the human suffering he saw around him. Or think about how the origin stories shared by Jews, Christians, and Muslims continue from the Creation of the world to yet another crucial decision to move—this time by Abram, who is called by God to leave Ur in Mesopotamia. That remarkable journey transforms him from Abram (exalted father) into Abraham (exalted father of multitudes), still a great patriarch for Jews and Christians. Muslims share a similar reverence but call him "Ibrahim," a prophet and messenger in the sacred line that leads to the Prophet Muhammad.

As you join me in the pages of this book, we will explore many forms of travel—from wonderful vacations, tours, and mission trips, which have been major milestones in our lives, to far more somber journeys like prison visitation or pilgrimages to remember tragedies like the Holocaust. We will consider travel that is voluntary—as well as travel that is involuntary, because our own American story includes both kinds. I was inspired to write this book in part because our collective love of tourism is again reaching all-time highs after the COVID years. But if we travel far in this world, we cannot escape the full range of what travel represents. Even as we travel to many American historical and cultural landmarks, we are reminded that millions had little choice about their travel.

Just one example: Since the United States Civil Rights Trail was founded on Martin Luther King Jr. Day in 2018, thousands of individuals and families have traveled among those 130 designated historical and cultural sites across fifteen states. Among those traveling families are men and women who are going home—and are taking their children and grandchildren home with them. For nearly four hundred years, the transatlantic slave trade brought as many as fifteen million men, women, and children from Africa to the Americas as enslaved people, the largest forced migration in human history.

Another example: Since the National Park Service Trail of Tears National Historic Trail was expanded in 2009, thousands of men, women, and children have devoted their vacation time to retracing that tragic route. The number of those travelers is expected to grow dramatically because May 2030 will be the 200th anniversary of the Indian Removal Act, sponsored by U.S. President Andrew Jackson, which forced Choctaw, Creek, Cherokee, and other Native Americans from their ancestral homelands in North Carolina, Tennessee, Georgia, and Alabama—to far more desolate patches of land that were set aside for Native Americans in what is now the state of Oklahoma. Some 100,000 people were forcibly relocated in a march that was over a thousand miles long, leaving in its wake countless loved ones who perished before they reached the western reservation.

All of this is our American story—from the joy of visiting the natural wonders in our most spectacular national parks to remembrances of the involuntary movement of people throughout our history.

If you picked up this book thinking that it might be about choosing future destinations for your vacations—well, we will definitely consider a few of them. But, as you must realize by now, that word "travel" means a great deal more than cruises, resorts, events, and good food. There are many spiritual, moral, and cultural questions about travel that are guaranteed to spark a good discussion series among your friends or members of your congregation.

In fact, this debate about the expanded definition of "travel" continues to be a controversial subject at annual conferences that bring together scholars of travel. And, yes, there are academics who research and argue about the ever-changing meaning of travel in its various forms. Thanks to Susan L. Roberson, a multidisciplinary scholar at Texas A&M University-Kingsville, you can read nearly two dozen of those academic viewpoints from around the world in a book of essays she titled *Defining Travel: Diverse Visions*, published by the University of Mississippi Press.

Among those with a stake in the great adventure explored in this book are sociologists, anthropologists, political scientists, and many other scholars, especially those who study timely issues involving women, religious movements, criminal justice, and indigenous rights. Nearly all of these researchers and educators are pushing for an expansion of the umbrella term "travel." That's because "travel" as a category for research and publication has been limited for far too long in a way that celebrates travel as "privilege," dominated by white, Western, and (all too often) male perspectives. That limited definition remains popular, partly because it meshes so conveniently with the multi-trillion-dollar—yes, *trillion*-dollar—tourism industry. Marketing tours, travel equipment, and vacation amenities to consumers are all about selling the dream of happy times in distant lands.

Only by expanding the definition of travel will millions of overlooked voices in our communities find the space to tell stories of women, the poor, indigenous, refugees, and incarcerated peoples.

Or to put it in Christian terms—to give voice to those who Jesus, in Matthew 25, commends to our care as "the least of these." The hungry, the thirsty, the stranger, the unclothed, the prisoner—all have their own stories of transformation through travel.

That's a central message in Roberson's *Defining Travel*. She opens her book by summarizing what we already know. We all agree on the basic "connection between travel and the construction of identity," as she puts it. Then, she summarizes her co-authors' call to break down barriers on what should be published in "travel" media. If we open our eyes and our resulting discussions, Roberson argues, there is a great deal we can discover.

One more example: Expanding our definition of travel allows us to ask questions from dual perspectives—both from the point of view of "visitors" as well as "the visited." How often do we return home after a big trip, sharing only the first version of that dual story?

In her introduction to the book, Roberson argues that what is truly exciting today is embracing the "multidimensionality of travel." As she puts it, "The field of travel itself 'travels' across academic and theoretical boundaries, bringing together sociology, anthropology, geography, history, psychology, and literary criticism." Roberson, like me, was inspired by the prophetic voice of William Least Heat-Moon to bust through traditional boundaries in studying travel. Reading Heat-Moon's work, especially, helped Roberson to realize that the whole notion of "mobility, too, is mobile."

Abram, Minnie, and me

So, let's return to that timeless companion of travel: storytelling.

If we want to explore travel in these new, expanded ways, then we have to share our stories—that's the whole point of this new worldwide effort. So, to inspire you to share your own accounts, I have packed this book with of a huge range of travel stories—pilgrimages, mission trips, prison visitation, career moves, vacations, and more. I am sharing my stories in the hope that they will spark memories of your own journeys and moves. As the novelist and memoirist Frederick Buechner writes in his book *Telling Secrets*, it is through telling our stories "in all their particularity … that God makes himself known." I would add that in telling our stories we also discover how much we have in common as children of God.

When God called Abram to leave his home in what is now Iraq, Abram went because God told him to go—apparently without questioning the command or asking where he was going. God described the destination to Abram simply as "the land I will show you," which turned out to be Canaan (what is now Israel, the West Bank and Gaza, Jordan, and the southern portions of Syria and Lebanon). So, Abram set out with his wife, Sarai, his nephew Lot, his possessions, and what the Bible curiously calls "the people they had acquired in Haran." Slaves? Other family members? It's not clear, but it must have been a large group of travelers.

They traveled west, most likely along the trade routes of the time, and then the Bible reports that "they arrived there." In other words, they arrived at the place God had in mind for Abram. Were they tired from the journey? Undoubtedly. Relieved to have arrived? Maybe, though wary, too, as all travelers tend to be in unfamiliar places. In other words, a long journey, and then—as countless others have discovered over the centuries—the even longer and sometimes disorienting task of looking around, meeting people, and making a new home.

We often read that account from Genesis without stopping to ask: Why did Abram go? He seems to have had a good life. He had accumulated a great deal of wealth. And yet he left at God's command for a place he had never seen. In doing so, he became a part of the grand epic of movement that defines the Hebrew Bible:

God's people moving, moving, moving—and God moving with them.

And all of that moving around in the ancient world raises questions, many of which can be found in scripture, from the Torah through the Psalms and even the prophets: How should we travel? How should we expect to be welcomed? How should we welcome others? And, at the end of our travels, can we expect a new home?

For me, these questions are as personal as the story of my grandmother Minnie.

Jacomina Glerum was five years old when she and her family set sail from the Netherlands on the Holland-America ocean liner SS Potsdam. At the time it was the largest ship in the Holland-America fleet, but ocean voyages in those days were not without peril. Still, my grandmother and her family set out. They arrived safely at Ellis Island on September 3, 1907. I know this because my grandmother told me about the journey, and much later in my life I investigated the story further, discovering through research many of the details she had forgotten or that I had neglected to ask her about.

Before leaving the Netherlands, her parents changed her name from Jacomina to Minnie, apparently a pet name they had given her. Minnie must have sounded more American to them, easier for Americans to pronounce and less likely to invite laughter or derision. As it turned out, there would be plenty of laughter and derision about other things, such as her clothes and accent. One of the playground taunts she remembered late in her life was, "Dutchman, Dutchman, belly full of straw, can't say nothin' but ja, ja, ja."

Many other immigrants, from the Netherlands and elsewhere, made a similar decision, taking entirely new names or changing the spelling of their old names. I had always assumed that uncaring immigration officials at Ellis Island changed the names of new immigrants, but to my surprise my grandmother's name on the ship manifest is clearly given as Minnie. She became Minnie before she boarded the ship, and she remained Minnie for the rest of her life.

More than thirty-four million Europeans, including my grandmother and her family, came to the U.S. in the nineteenth and early twentieth centuries in one of the largest migrations on record. Though many of them left voluntarily, eager to make a new start on another continent, many of them were also motivated by economic circumstances. More than a million people, for example, migrated from Ireland to the U.S. (as well as Canada and Australia) between 1841 and 1850 to avoid a deadly famine.

Leaving one's home country, saying goodbye to family and friends, changing one's name, embarking on a sometimes-perilous ocean voyage, not knowing what the future holds—I have always wondered why anyone would do this. But I have come to see that a better question is: Why have *so many* people throughout history done this? Why do they *continue* to do it? And, because they have made these journeys, how has that made their lives different?

I have also done a fair amount of setting out and moving around in my own life—always voluntarily, never in desperation—and I know those travels around our planet have indelibly shaped my life in many ways, sometimes in ways I never expected or even realized fully at the time. Now, though, I wonder if I truly understood why I set out on those journeys, beyond the plausible explanations I gave to people at the time. More importantly, I wonder how the yearnings that stirred me through these travels transformed me afterward.

That is the wonderment into which I am inviting you as this book unfolds—to reflect on your own travels and those of your close friends and loved ones. Why did we set out? What drew us out—or pushed us to go? How did we think about that at the time? And, upon further reflection over the years, have we truly been honest about why we set out? Then, with the benefit of time, how did those decisions forever mark our lives?

If we honestly consider these questions together, we are likely to discover a truth we share in these stories. While we may think we are in charge of our vacations, mission trips, pilgrimages, professional moves, and other migrations we may be part of, on a deeper level in these life transitions we often are "getting lost to find ourselves." And, yes, I know: Sometimes that truth may take years to discern—and that is why I invite you to start on this journey by looking back in your own life—perhaps way back, depending on your age.

Unlike my grandmother, I was nearly twenty-one years old when I left home for the first time. The summer before setting out was filled with equal amounts of anticipation and anxiety, and I finally left in September for an exotic place known as New Jersey, 750 miles to the east of where I was born and raised. I knew no one there, and no one knew me. I had a letter of admission from Princeton Theological Seminary in Princeton, New Jersey, but I had never been to the seminary and had never spoken to a single person there. I had not even taken a campus tour, which any prospective student today would insist on doing. I knew little about the school and even less about New Jersey, but based on the little I knew, I wanted to go—to see and explore and experience.

I set out by car, not steamship, and everything I owned and considered valuable was in that car—including a houseplant that a girlfriend insisted on sending along with me. It was the first big journey of my life. I had had other, much smaller adventures before this one, but this was one of those where I knew I was going all in. In my mind I had pushed all my chips to the center of the table. I figured that I would either succeed—whatever that meant—or die trying.

My experience turned out to be far more difficult than I had ever imagined, and yet from the distance of a few decades I can say that it was also far better than I had ever imagined. My grandmother, toward the end of her life, expressed something similar during one of our conversations. Coming to a new country was hard, she said, unspeakably hard at times, but she could not imagine having lived her life differently. There were days, she said, when she desperately missed what she called the "old country," but she never seriously thought about going back. Most days I have that same feeling. I do not regret having set out. I suppose I would do it all over again.

When I left home for the first time, I knew that most people in New Jersey spoke English, so I figured that language would not be an obstacle. I was wrong about that and much else. I noticed from the first day that people in New Jersey spoke English, but they used a different dialect, vocabulary, and rhythm in their speech. People sounded different. And I sounded different to them with my Midwestern diction. I was surprised by how little I really knew about New Jersey. And very quickly, I realized that the people I met knew little about me. Most did not even recognize the name of the college I had graduated from.

Someone in New Jersey had sent me a letter of admission and had promised me a room on campus where I would be allowed to live, and so based on two short paragraphs—printed on impressive-looking stationery—I set out.

In the case of Abram—who, like my grandmother, underwent a name change as part of his journey—we are told that he set out for Canaan because he obeyed God, and ever since he has been known as a hero of faith, a model of obedience. That's not the whole story, of course, but that's how we usually remember him. Abraham, as he became known, made some questionable decisions after his decision to obey God's command (twice he tried passing off his wife as his sister when his hosts took an interest in her), but according to the story nothing he did would ever diminish his singular act of faithfulness. God told him to go, and he did.

As a child I was told that when God told Abraham to go, God commanded him to "be a blessing." In fact, God said to Abraham, "In you all the nations of the world shall be blessed." In graduate study I learned that these statements are far more complicated, even problematic, than I presumed. Still, my childhood faith took the command to "be a blessing" at face value. I assumed that in moving around, like Abraham, I was expected to "be a blessing." And so, that's what I set out to be.

With that move to New Jersey, it now seems clear that, like my grandmother, I wasn't going back to the old country, that a pattern had been established, that I would spend much of my life setting out and meeting people and making a new home for myself.

When *Sehnsucht* sparks a 'worthy adventure'

All of this moving around that people do, this longing to see and experience new things, this vague dissatisfaction with where we find ourselves right now, can be described in another, perhaps better, way.

Sehnsucht is a German term with such a precise meaning that most translators make no attempt to render it into English. *Sehnsucht* is a yearning for something that we can't quite define, a feeling of incompleteness that drives us to search for something more, a feeling of dissatisfaction with the present that compels us to seek something more fulfilling. C.S. Lewis once described *Sehnsucht* as an "inconsolable longing" in the human heart for "we know not what." At least two other languages have words that also refer to a longing we can't quite describe, which points, I believe, to the universality of the concept.

I have come to see that this inconsolable longing for "we know not what" is spiritual. It is, we might say, a yearning for God.

As humans with spiritual callings that we may choose to act on—or ignore—that choice of deciding where to go each day, especially whether to leave home on a grander journey, can take many forms. Sometimes, travel is all but forced upon us. Sometimes, we feel that we are in charge of these plans. And, sometimes, our journeys may even approach the magnitude of what the ethicist Stanley Hauerwas likes to call a "worthy adventure." To Hauerwas, a worthy adventure is something that gives our lives meaning and purpose, but not just any old adventure. For an adventure to be worthy, as he puts it, it must be something worth dying for, something that challenges us to grow and learn and connect with others, something worthy of the gifts and abilities we have been given.

Hauerwas wants us to understand all of life as a worthy adventure, and it's true that, every time we get up in the morning, we can think of the day ahead in terms of an adventure. It can be healthy and even exciting to live that way. With that intention—to live life as an adventure—everything that happens to us is an opportunity to grow, and every person we meet can enrich our lives. We can even frame life's inevitable disappointments and setbacks as occasions for growth and change. I would like to think that most days I live that way.

For the purpose of this book, though, "worthy adventure" will refer to something narrower, something more than what happens with each new day. A worthy adventure takes us outside our comfort zones. It often involves risk since the outcome is unknown. It can be a physical challenge, such as deciding to run a marathon or climb a mountain. It can be a spiritual challenge, such as studying a new religion or getting a degree in one's own faith tradition. It can be a creative challenge, such as starting a business or writing a book. All of those seem like fine adventures. I have attempted more than one of them. But the sort of adventure I have in mind here, the kind I am describing as "worthy," not only helps us to grow but changes the way we think about ourselves. Not superficially, but deeply and profoundly.

The sort of adventure I have in mind is also more than an exercise in self-fulfillment. It can be that too, of course, and I see nothing wrong in seeking self-fulfillment. But for an adventure to be worthy, it should change me and it should change others. Perhaps I should use the language of being "other directed." In other words, a worthy adventure is never only about us. We will be changed, but the people we meet will be changed as well. Abraham, as I was taught, was to "be a blessing." And, in fact, Abraham's life ultimately changed many lives across many generations—including yours and mine.

As we set out on an adventure through these pages, I hope you will find many more of these deeply personal connections—as I did when I discovered that the scholar Susan Roberson was as deeply moved by the writing of William Least Heat-Moon as I was. All too often we think of our experiences with our most beloved authors as, well, ours. I now know Heat-Moon's words have touched many lives, mainly through *Blue Highways*, the account of his own worthy adventure, which found itself on *The New York Times* bestseller list for forty-two weeks.

In 1978, at the age of thirty-eight, soon after losing his ten-year marriage and his teaching job, Heat-Moon set out in his Ford van (which he christened "Ghost Dancing") on an adventure that covered more than thirteen thousand miles around the United States. The journey started as more of a desperate escape from his old life than any kind of a worthy adventure. "A man who couldn't make things go right could at least go," he writes in the opening paragraphs. Never on interstate highways, always on back roads (hence the name of the book), Heat-Moon discovered a country that most of us never see—or take time to see.

What makes his adventure more than a log of his thirteen thousand miles is that Heat-Moon was changed along the way, in ways he could not have imagined when he first set out. "Time is not the traveler's fourth dimension—change is," he writes. The book is not so much about him as it is about the people he met along the way, the conversations he had with them, and the tenderness he would often share with the least likely people—a Seventh-Day Adventist, an evangelical hitchhiker, a teenage runaway, a boat builder, a monk, an Appalachian log cabin restorer, a rural Nevada sex worker, a Hopi Native American medical student, owners of saloons and remote country stores, a maple syrup farmer, and lots of fishermen. Each one of these encounters seems to have affected Heat-Moon in different ways, but as he listened, he grew in understanding—of himself and his country.

Heat-Moon claims no religious affiliation, but his story is deeply spiritual. People who do the work of pastoral counseling and spiritual direction often cite the book as an inspiration and example for their own work. His experiences profoundly affected the people he met, and his story continues to have that effect on readers today.

I call that a worthy adventure.

I would like to think that reading this book will become a worthy adventure for all of us—for me, as your narrator and guide, and for you as you ponder the connections in your own movements around our planet. My hope is that this book might prompt you to set out and see something new, a place where you, too, can be changed—and of course "be a blessing" to others.

2

The Gift of Curiosity

"It was my life—like all lives, mysterious and irrevocable and sacred. So very close, so very present, so very belonging to me. How wild it was, to let it be."

**Cheryl Strayed,
Wild: From Lost to Found on the Pacific Crest Trail**

My parents gave me the gift of curiosity.

My earliest memory of summer vacation is loading suitcases into the trunk of our car and setting off with Mom, Dad, and my sisters for three-week road trips across the United States and Canada. Driving five hundred to six hundred miles in one day was not uncommon. My family was determined to see as much of the lower forty-eight states and Canada as it was humanly possible to see. And we saw a lot.

We saw canyons and mountains and waterfalls, we visited the boyhood homes of U.S. presidents, we saw (and swam in) the Pacific Ocean, the Atlantic Ocean, and the Gulf of Mexico, and we were even in the studio audience once for a taping of the old TV game show *Truth or Consequences*, hosted by Bob Barker.

The Space Needle in Seattle was completed in December 1961, and not many months later we were there staring up at it. We rode the elevator 605 feet to the top and had lunch in the restaurant which rotated 360 degrees every hour. I had tuna salad on toast and thought it was an elegant dining experience. In 1964, we traveled to New York City to see the World's Fair. Soon after the Houston Astrodome was built in 1965 we took an afternoon tour of this "eighth wonder of the world," as the guide referred to it, and then saw a professional baseball game that night. One summer we traveled to Florida and toured Cape Canaveral, the place where the Mercury, Gemini, and Apollo spacecrafts were assembled and launched. The Vehicle Assembly Building, which is exactly 4.2 miles from the launchpad, was so large that it created its own weather inside—or so the guide informed us. Another summer we visited the Civil War battlefield and museum near Gettysburg, Pennsylvania. Today, my children and grandchildren would be bored by the showpiece of our visit, the Cyclorama—an immersive painting of the battle that surrounded us and presented the various skirmishes and charges along with electric lights and sound effects—but it affected me in a very vivid way.

We never camped. We stayed instead at Holiday Inns when we could find them, and there always seemed to be a lot of them along the way. This may explain why I never camp today. As a kid, I loved the Holiday Inn swimming pools—such a welcome relief after a long day packed in the car. We ate all of our meals in restaurants. Not quite luxury travel, but close to it.

The best part of these adventures was that we didn't just see places and things. We met people, too. Lots of them. We once visited a missionary family in Gallup, New Mexico, and learned of their work with Zuni and Navajo people. We stopped to see one of Dad's high school classmates who had moved to Los Angeles. We even went to church on Sundays, trying hard to find congregations along the way from the tiny denomination of my childhood. Imagine finding a Dutch Reformed congregation in the heart of Mormon country. One Sunday morning, we worshipped in the living room of a pastor's home in Salt Lake City.

Much of this travel, I suspect, was for my benefit. My sisters had no interest in either baseball stadiums or the boyhood homes of U.S. presidents, but they never complained. The only complaints

I heard were about our personal space in the backseat of the car, three children trying not to touch each other on a long day of driving. Somehow my sisters and I passed time without screens to look at, which seems remarkable to me now. Instead, we read books, and we looked at cornfields and mountain ranges—and often license plates on the cars we passed. An annual summer challenge was to find license plates from all fifty states by the time we returned home. We were usually at forty-seven or forty-eight at only a hundred miles from home, making for a frantic search over the last stretch of highway.

One summer, Dad made me the trip accountant and gave me a ledger for travel expenses. He passed on to me every restaurant and motel and gas receipt, and I did my best to keep track of our expenses. I was even able to calculate the mileage our car was getting—which wasn't very good by today's standards. What my dad did with my bookkeeping at the end of the trip, I don't know. My guess is that he was probably trying to give me something to do while we drove.

Dad did all of the driving, typically thousands of miles, and he seemed to find it relaxing. I don't remember Mom ever driving, not even for a few miles. Dad always had one arm at the open window (in the years before air conditioning in cars was standard), which meant that he returned home every summer with one very tan arm. Mom was always the navigator and the one who passed out occasional treats. My sisters and I did our best to be quiet and not fight. One time—somewhere out West—I was in the backseat immediately behind Dad and made the sound of a tire rapidly losing air, which I thought was quite funny. Dad, however, was not amused, particularly not later that same day when one of our tires actually went flat. After that one attempt at humor, I never made car noises again.

Dad was an artist and always seemed to have a camera around his neck during those vacations. Photography was one of his few hobbies, and our trips were an opportunity for him to enjoy something he loved. He was partial to Nikon cameras with multiple lenses, and over the years he brought back thousands of photos. Soon after we came home from one of our trips, he would bring his rolls of film to a camera store to be developed. Late into the evening he would organize the slides (never prints) into the carousel tray of a Kodak slide projector. We would see the slide show once, and then the trays disappeared into a closet, although I now realize that his slides were often the inspirations for his paintings.

To this day, I do wonder why Dad never took typical family photos. There's no record of us grouped along the rim of the Grand Canyon, for example. What interested Dad was not creating a record of where we went, but a catalog of beautiful sunsets, flowers (often in extreme closeups), mountains, and old buildings, especially barns. He thought of his photography as art—or at least an inspiration for his art.

I would often bring along a camera of my own, and what I learned from Dad was to see the world the way he saw it, to find beauty, to look for the best angle and the most interesting perspective. The purpose was not to say, "Hey, look at me! I'm in the Smokey Mountains!" The purpose, which never needed an explanation, was that I was there to see and appreciate and remember.

When I graduated from high school, the days of summer road trips came to an end. My older sister had left home for school and then marriage. And my younger sister seemed pleased not to have to continue the road-trip tradition as an only child. My parents asked me what I wanted for a graduation present, hoping that I would ask for an electric typewriter for college term papers, and I surprised them—and to some degree myself—by saying that I wanted to go to Europe.

My thinking at the time wasn't clear. This was years before the internet, and I had no idea how anyone got around in Europe or purchased a "Eurail pass" or found youth hostels for overnights, though I knew that other young people were doing those things. All I knew was that "backpacking through Europe" sounded adventurous, which is what I wanted to be. I didn't really expect that my parents would allow their seventeen-year-old son to backpack through Europe, and to be honest I never developed much of a plan. It was the idea, the delight in saying it out loud, that I enjoyed. I wanted to be the kind of person who would set out into the unknown with nothing more than a backpack and see the world.

What happened was a shock. I was given the electric typewriter anyway. And then—my parents announced that they were taking my younger sister and me on a three-week tour of European capitals, starting a week after my high school graduation. That's how I acquired my first passport at the age of seventeen. I would be going to Europe, and I would be staying in hotels, not hostels. One of the high points of my young life.

The tour we took was sponsored by the alumni association at the college I would be attending. There were thirty to forty people in the group, and we traveled in a large, air-conditioned tour bus. The itinerary was full, except, as I recall, for one "free afternoon" in Amsterdam toward the end of our three weeks. Meals, overnights, entrance fees for museums—everything was taken care of by a tour company. The euro would not be introduced for another twenty-two years, and so we accumulated lots of Dutch guilders, Italian lira, German marks, and French francs along the way. I still have some of those coins somewhere.

Our guide was a young woman in her thirties, and I developed quite a crush on her. I probably blushed when, after a stop, she would walk through the bus to count heads. She was smart and pretty, and she spoke several languages, which at the time deeply impressed me. I had never known anyone like her. Also, as we were leaving Paris, I remember that she said—over the bus's PA system—"There's an old saying that 'every time you leave Paris, you die a little.'" These words have been attributed to Simone de Beauvoir, though there is no evidence that she actually spoke them. Still, imagine being able to make a sophisticated comment like that. I wanted some of what she had.

We saw cathedrals (so many cathedrals), museums (so many paintings), as well as lots of quaint medieval towns and villages. For some reason, though, Michelangelo's David was not on the itinerary, and Dad was not about to visit Europe without seeing that famous sculpture. So, in Florence we hailed a taxi, sped over to the Accademia Gallery of Florence, and stood a good while with the statue, while the rest of the group ate lunch. Our guide warned us before we left that the bus would not wait if we were delayed in noontime traffic, but she also winked at us and said, "I would do the same thing." We made it back to the group with a few minutes to spare, and while our little excursion doesn't rank very high on any risk-taking scale, I began to see why risk-taking could be so thrilling.

The most jarring part of our tour was seeing the Berlin Wall and Checkpoint Charlie. At the checkpoint, where we crossed from West to East Berlin, we were required to get off the bus while the interior was searched and large mirrors on wheels were rolled underneath the bus. I'm not sure what a group like ours might attempt to smuggle into East Berlin, but soon we re-boarded the bus and rolled through the Iron Curtain and into East Germany. I remember that the bus was quiet that afternoon with faces pressed against the windows. Not many Americans were allowed to see life behind the Iron Curtain. My own memory is that, except for the barbed wire and armed guards at the checkpoint, life seemed surprisingly normal. Even then, though, I knew we were seeing what the East German government was permitting us to see.

Nurturing the adventurous spirit

After I started college, my parents continued to travel. They returned to Europe a few more times. They also went to Hawaii (where my dad was stationed during World War II), Israel, Mexico, Argentina, Japan, the Soviet Union, and even China. Not long after Richard Nixon's historic visit to the Peoples' Republic in 1971, tourists began to visit the country, and among them—no surprise to me—were my parents. At the age of 88, after two surgeries for spinal stenosis that made walking difficult, Dad was still hoping one day to explore India. Sadly for him, that day never came. And both of my parents are now gone.

My parents maintained their adventurous spirit throughout their lives. What puzzles me is that they were curious about some things—like art and geography—but not others. My parents were raised in a religious tradition with strong sectarian impulses, and therefore they were suspicious of other churches and their teachings. Their own childhoods were the opposite of mine. As children they seldom, if ever, left West Michigan. Dad left after high school to serve in World War II—with the U.S. Navy Seabees, the construction battalion—but returned home as soon as the war ended. Like most members of his generation, he never spoke about those years.

My decision a few years after college to become a Presbyterian and to leave the Dutch Reformed church of my childhood was difficult for them to accept. To their credit, they did their best to understand, but their intellectual curiosity was never quite as wide-ranging as their curiosity about other things. They always were eager to see the latest art exhibit, but never to hear what a Presbyterian preacher (other than their son) might have to say.

There were other limits to their adventurous spirit—for example, their preference to see the world through the windows of a tour bus.

Whenever they left the North American continent, they preferred the safety and predictability of a guide, tour group, and printed itinerary. After that first tour of Europe with my parents, however, I would not ride a bus again, except for Holy Land pilgrimages.

So, how did my parents give me this gift of curiosity?

By global standards, I realize that our ability to travel was a privilege that millions around the world do not enjoy. On the other hand, the five of us lived in a modest, four-bedroom, one-bathroom ranch house in a suburb. My parents made a choice—exploring the world over saving their money for a more expensive house.

I have inherited similar values. But how?

Based on my reading of the scientific literature, an adventurous spirit can have both a genetic component and an environmental cause—a combination of nature and nurture. Scientific debate still swirls around a gene known as DRD4, which has been called an "adventure" gene. Some studies suggest variants of DRD4 may have pushed some populations down through history to migrate across long distances. Others claim that this gene may play a role in a person's level of "novelty seeking" in general—restlessly wanting to encounter new things and places. However, the latest studies of DRD4 raise more questions than answers. It seems that, if an instinct to travel can be handed down biologically, then it's through a more complex pattern than just one genetic strand. And that leaves us with the second way we might inherit a thirst for adventure: By growing up in families that encourage exploration and risks associated with travel. That certainly makes sense to me—except that my sisters, who had the same experiences I did throughout childhood, do not share my strong urge to move around and explore the world. They have lived most of their lives within a few miles of where we grew up. In the end, there's still mystery in the impulses that push some of us to travel far and wide.

Gender can also be a factor in adventurousness. Historically, men have been more likely than women to engage in risk-taking behavior—like sky diving, say, or bungee jumping. But this seems to be changing, indicating that social norms may have been the real reason that women have not engaged in as much risk-taking behavior as men.

I read recently about a woman who grew up, as I did, in West Michigan and graduated from a Dutch Reformed college like mine. Jenn Drummond has now climbed all "seven second summits"—all seven of the second-highest peaks on every continent. It's a remarkable achievement, involving a great deal of risk taking. In one newspaper profile, Jenn attributes her impulse to a car accident earlier in her life. Her car was struck by a tractor trailer and turned over three times before coming to rest. "I closed my eyes," she remembers thinking in the overturned car, "and I could wiggle my fingers and toes, and I go, 'I can feel my fingers and toes; I'm okay.'" It's quite a story, and maybe there are occasions when a traumatic experience prompts us to seek adventure, to take risks, to remind ourselves of the preciousness of life. But even trauma cannot fully explain why some of us do what we do.

A family member likes to challenge me on what he calls my romanticization of adventure. It's not that he's never gone anywhere, but he wonders if my fondness for setting out and going places and experiencing new things isn't based on something else, maybe a dislike for where I grew up or the sometimes-suffocating community in which I was raised. What if I seek out adventures because I am unhappy with where I am? It's a fair question, and many writers have reflected on it. Charles Baudelaire, the nineteenth century French poet, once famously exclaimed, "The destination was not really the point. The true desire was to get away—to go ... 'anywhere!' 'anywhere!' so long as it is out in the world." Baudelaire had a complex relationship with France. He was born and raised in Paris, and he loved the city's beauty and cultural vitality, but he was also critical of the country's political and social institutions. In his poem "Le Voyage," Baudelaire writes about his desire to escape from France and travel to exotic lands like Egypt.

I understand that impulse. When I first loaded up my car and headed to Princeton, New Jersey, I was glad to be leaving West Michigan. I loved the beauty of the place, but at the same time found it suffocating. I would not have been able then to put much of this into words, but I remember thinking that to grow up I needed to leave. How was I to know who I was and what I believed in a culture that valued sameness and conformity over exploration and discovery?

To my relative who likes to challenge me about my desire for adventure, I say, "I could be wrong, but I keep thinking there is *more* out there. And I would like to see, taste, and experience it."

3

Does Travel Make Us Better People?

*"Adventure is not outside man;
it is within."*

George Eliot, Middlemarch: A Study of Provincial Life

Based on my childhood experience—those long summer road trips—I assumed that everyone loved to set out and go somewhere as much as I do. I also assumed that everyone who travels would be admired for doing it. Don't we mean it as a compliment when we describe someone as "well traveled"? I used to.

But what if travel isn't inherently a good thing? What if it doesn't always lead to the outcomes that we often claim for it? What if travel is in many ways seriously flawed, something that should be reconsidered? What if most travel isn't what Stanley Hauerwas would describe as "worthy adventure"?

I forget how old I was when I realized that there is a great deal to dislike about travel. In fact, I can think of lots of reasons these days to stay home and not go anywhere. Just getting to an airport gate can be a daunting exercise. And the work of getting ready to travel begins long before the day of departure. To go anywhere means stopping the mail, finding someone to mow the lawn, and (for longer trips) asking a neighbor to come over and start my car once a week. And that's just the beginning. Then there is the inevitable exhaustion of travel itself, arriving bleary-eyed at a foreign airport and trying to find your way, after finally getting through passport control and baggage claim. More than one person has arrived at a destination and thought, "Was that really worth it?"

Turns out that there is much more that can be mentioned—beyond the long checklist of things to do—when offering a critique of travel. Agnes Callard, a University of Chicago philosopher, in a *New Yorker* essay title "The Case Against Travel," disagrees with the premise that travel is inherently valuable, that travel changes us and makes us better people, that the hassle of getting somewhere is always worth the rich experience that a traveler inevitably has. On the contrary, she argues that "the traveler departs confident that she will come back with the same basic interests, political beliefs, and living arrangements." In other words, in her view, travel leaves most of us utterly unchanged.

"Tourism"—you can sense Callard's derisive tone when she uses this word—amounts to little more than "locomotion." Here's how she puts it: "'I *went* to France.' O.K., but what did you do there? 'I *went* to the Louvre.' O.K., but what did you do there? 'I *went* to see the Mona Lisa.' That is, before quickly moving on [because] apparently many people spend just fifteen seconds looking at the Mona Lisa."

Having spent much of my life going places and regarding those experiences as inherently worthwhile, sometimes lifechanging, I very much wanted to understand this particular case against travel. After reading Callard's essay, I am ready to acknowledge that there is a solid case to be made against much of the travel that people say they enjoy, maybe even against most travel.

Frankly, I was unaware that anyone detested travel quite as much as Callard, having grown up the way I did, but I should have anticipated that there would be a different point of view. There nearly always is. Callard even cites an impressive number of thinkers and writers in history who have made the case that travel doesn't do much of anything for us. G.K. Chesterton, the

English writer and philosopher, once claimed that "travel narrows the mind," while most people I know argue the opposite. Ralph Waldo Emerson, the American essayist, called travel "a fool's paradise." Socrates and Immanuel Kant, two of the most formidable philosophers in history, rarely left their hometowns of Athens and Königsberg. Samuel Johnson, still another English writer, once wrote that "what I gained by being in France was learning to be better satisfied with my own country." And there are more.

Just when I would like to dismiss Callard as a contrarian—and she does have something of a contrarian reputation, though that can be a strength in her field and has arguably made her a thoughtful and original thinker—I confess that much of what she writes is true. For example, she writes that at home we tend to avoid "touristy" activities and places that we describe as "tourist traps." All the various uses of the word "tourist," she notes, tend to be negative. "Tourism," she explains, is almost always what other people do, and we almost never want to hear much about their travels or see their many photos posted on social media.

Cities in Europe like Venice, Amsterdam, Barcelona, and Bruges have rightly been described as "over-touristed," meaning that they have been overrun with tourists, especially during certain months of the year. There is something sad and even troubling about a once-beautiful city that today functions more like an amusement park than a city. Today much of the population in Venice and Bruges is made up of nonnatives—tourists, second homeowners, or people who have moved to those cities for work. Only about fifty-five percent of the population in Venice is native Venetian, and in Bruges the percentage is an astonishingly low forty percent.

"Travel," she concludes, "gets branded as an achievement: see interesting places, have interesting experiences, become interesting people. Is that what it really is?" The answer, I concede, is no. Much of the time travel is not the achievement it has become in the popular imagination.

Callard, as it turns out, is not the first travel contrarian to publish in a major publication. More than a hundred years ago, in June 1911, the *Atlantic Monthly* published an essay titled "The Immorality of Travel," which goes even further than Callard does. "Travel," the author claimed, "is the great epidemic of the modern world … wasteful of time and money, disastrous to the places visited, most unbeautiful in all its effects."

If travel more than a hundred years ago already was becoming a kind of global plague, then the situation today can only be described as far worse. When the *Atlantic* published that unsigned contribution, the writer was railing against the frustrations of travel in a world still limited by ships and trains. Roadways for cars were in their infancy; airliners were a fantasy of the future. Ellis Island had seen its busiest single year in 1907 with a total that astonished Americans: 1.25 million immigrants. But today? Pew Research reports that nearly four out of five people in our world of eight billion have traveled to at least one other country.

Sorting the luggage we carry: bigotry, awe, and fear

Can you imagine that number reported by Pew? More than six billion souls have engaged in some form of international travel.

Were many of them changed by what they did?

Some people love to cite the Mark Twain quote in which he extols the virtues of travel. The famous words are found toward the end of his well-known travel book *Innocents Abroad*. "Travel," he writes in his conclusion, "is fatal to prejudice, bigotry, and narrow-mindedness, and many of our people need it sorely on these accounts. Broad, wholesome, charitable views of men and things cannot be acquired by vegetating in one little corner of the earth all one's lifetime."

Sounds good, doesn't it? I like those words and want them to be true. But after a recent rereading of the book, I wonder how much Twain learned during his own travels.

In 1867, two newspapers, the *New York Tribune* and San Francisco's *Daily Alta California*, organized a group of sixty passengers to travel on a chartered steamship for five months to Europe and (what travel planners still like to call) the Holy Land. Twain used his connections to secure a place on board, and in 1869 *Innocents Abroad*, an account of that trip, was published. The book helped establish Twain's reputation as one of the most talented writers of his time.

Here's the thing, though: Much of the book makes me cringe. Far from being "fatal to prejudice," Twain's experience seems to have reinforced his views of other peoples and lands. Even taking into account Twain's unique brand of humor and the time in which he wrote, his descriptions of nonwhite people (and even a fair number of white people) can be described as awkward, uncomfortable, and racist.

Early in the book, before Twain reached the European mainland, the steamship he was traveling on stopped at an island in the Azores, near Portugal, and this is what he writes: "The community is eminently Portuguese—that is to say, it is slow, poor, shiftless, sleepy, and lazy. There is a civil governor, appointed by the King of Portugal, and also a military governor, who can assume supreme control and suspend the civil government at his pleasure. The islands contain a population of about 200,000, almost entirely Portuguese ... There is not a wheelbarrow in the land—they carry everything on their heads, or on donkeys, or in a wicker-bodied cart, whose wheels are solid blocks of wood and whose axles turn with the wheel. There is not a modern plow in the islands or a threshing machine. All attempts to introduce them have failed. The good Catholic Portuguese crossed himself and prayed God to shield him from all blasphemous desire to know more than his father did before him."

I wish I could report that this is the only example—or the worst one—but it isn't. It is difficult to escape the impression that, even though Twain wanted travel to be a broadening experience, it wasn't for him in the way that we would understand that desire today.

So, it is fair to ask: Does travel make us better people?

That's a question I will continue to ask as we make our way through the adventures in these chapters. My suspicion is that a positive answer most often includes a moment of awe.

Cultivating feelings of wonder about the world is what I remember most fondly from those early road trips with my family. When I caught my first glimpse of the Grand Canyon, I was stunned. Like all our family trips, I went with my parents and sisters, and somewhere in Arizona we stopped at a "scenic overlook" to get our first glimpse.

No photo will ever do it justice. I was overwhelmed. I was peering into something 277 "river miles" long and eighteen miles wide at its widest point. What amazes me is that the canyon is considered young, by geological standards, because much of it was eroded in the last five to six million years.

I vividly recall other moments of awe over many years. Seeing the aurora borealis over Iceland was overwhelming, for example, and I could list more such stunning moments. But, how about you?

Indigenous people were so moved by such moments that they ascribed religious meaning to these experiences. Climbing to the top of Machu Picchu, which stands more than seven thousand feet above sea level, inspires that same wonder. Why was this Incan citadel, set high in the Andes Mountains in what is now Peru, built in the fifteenth century and then abandoned? The walls fuse huge blocks without the use of mortar, and the buildings seem to play on astronomical alignments and panoramic views. All astonishing, but no one seems to know for sure why it was built or how it was used.

After reading Callard, though, I wondered if this openness to awe and wonder might be something I have convinced myself is true. Maybe a better measure of the worth of something is to ask, Am I different *as a result of* where I have been and what I have experienced? Has there been a noticeable change in my behavior? In other words, is anything at all about me different *as a result of* my "once in a lifetime" experience? Or to put the question differently, why do we often feel compelled to "imbue" (Callard's word) travel with "a vast significance"?

Isn't a vacation sometimes merely—a vacation?

In addition to moments of awe, I suspect that another telling detail in transformative travel is what Tim O'Brien, more than three decades ago, called *The Things They Carried*, about a platoon of American soldiers in the Vietnam War. And that's why I'm suggesting that we pause here to "sort the luggage we carry."

Unlike Agnes Callard, Rick Steves is one of the best-known proponents of travel in recent years. He has spent most of his adult life traveling and promoting travel. He has hosted *Rick Steves' Europe* for public television and is the author of several travel guidebooks. Among Steves' luggage is his long-time membership of the Evangelical Lutheran Church in America. Steves is someone who believes in and seeks out transformative experiences. In an interview with *The Christian Century*, Steves said, "People have a lot of fear. The flip side of fear is understanding. When you travel to places new to you, you understand more, so you fear less. And then you can love people, as a Christian should. The less you travel, the more likely that media with a particular agenda can shape your viewpoint. Those of us who travel are a little more resilient when it comes to weathering the propaganda storms that blow constantly across the U.S. media."

I believe this—and I want it to be true. I would like to think that travel increases our understanding of other people and cultures.

I still wonder how much understanding happens through the windows of a tour bus, but based on my own experiences, going places, seeing things, and getting out of our familiar and comfortable lives is an important first step toward understanding. Not all travelers, perhaps, but some of them will then take additional steps and want to meet and get to know the people and cultures they are seeing. Few people have done more than Rick Steves to promote and encourage this point of view, especially with his insistence that travelers avoid the major tourist destinations and find the less-traveled towns and villages of Europe.

Pico Iyer, who has written a great deal about crossing cultures, is still another important voice on this subject. In a recent book titled *The Half-Known Life*, Iyer defends the thesis that travel can be an antidote to fear and ignorance. "It seems to me," he writes, "that a lot of the problems we have today—racism, xenophobia, toxic nationalism—are because so many people have never been exposed to different peoples, cultures, and communities beyond their immediate world. Basically, they've never traveled. Do you think travel can be an antidote to the pervasive fear and hostility toward the other we see around the world?"

As I read his book, my answer was: I think so.

We will explore visits to the "Holy Land" later in this book, but relevant to this chapter is the awe I experienced in meeting Arab Christians the first time I visited Israel and the West Bank. From history classes I knew something about the Holocaust, the founding of the Israeli state, and the importance of Israel today to the worldwide Jewish diaspora. However, before that first in-person visit to the lands around Jerusalem, I knew little about Palestinians—and had no experience with the ancient Arab Christian communities in that region. Today, as a result of my travels, I count the noted interfaith peacemaker Elias Chacour as a friend. Before his retirement in 2014, he served as an archbishop in the Melkite Greek Catholic Church. Visiting him at the school he founded in I'billin and hearing him speak for the first time was a remarkable and lifechanging experience. His words so greatly expanded my understanding of the people in this region that I made sure to visit Father Chacour on each subsequent visit to Israel. I have been a guest at his home in I'billin—as well as the archbishop's residence in Haifa—and he has been a guest in my home in the U.S. I have read his books and heard his stories. I celebrated each time he was nominated for a Nobel Peace Prize. My world view, it is safe to say, has been changed because of meeting and getting to know him; my perspective on Israel and its founding has been enlarged. Israel was no longer a distant country, irrelevant to my life, but a place where I knew people and where those people knew me.

Another major figure who continues to challenge and expand my concepts of travel is the Trappist monk and bestselling author Thomas Merton. In fact, he spent most of his adult life at a small abbey in Kentucky, rarely straying from his abbey grounds partly because one of his long-time abbots forbade him to travel far. As a result, Merton did a great deal of reflecting and writing about the spiritual life, exploring ever-widening concentric circles of faith until he became world famous as a leading Christian interpreter of Buddhism. In his book *Mystics and Zen Masters*, he wrote that "the geographical pilgrimage is the symbolic acting out of an inner journey. The inner journey is the interpolation of the meanings and signs of the outer pilgrimage. One can have one without the other. It is best to have both."

Merton argues that the transformative power of travel is best understood when it is rooted in something happening within us. Many people look forward to seeing and experiencing something new, but they do not have the desire or the tools to explore further, to ask about the meaning of their outer journey.

As Merton points out, it is possible to have the outer journey without the inner, but I can affirm his conclusion: "It is best to have both."

And, in fact, it was not until the autumn of 1968, just weeks before his death in an electrical accident at a retreat facility in Thailand, that Merton was able to finally spend time deeply engaged with religious leaders in Asia—both Christian and non-Christian, including several meetings with the then-quite-young Dalai Lama. And it was only in an off-the-cuff talk he delivered to a mainly non-Christian crowd of religious leaders in Calcutta that Merton gave his most powerful affirmation of the way his two journeys—inner and outer—had transformed him. He began by joking about the luggage he carried—including the "Roman collar" he wore as if that somehow signified his role. In fact, he startled the crowd by calling his collar merely a "disguise." Most of them in attendance that day had arrayed themselves in all the finery, stoles, and riches that were signs of their ranks. Merton called on all of them to look past those things they carried. Only by looking past such trappings, he argued, could the men gathered all around him—and most were men in that gathering—hope to experience the deeper awe of that gathering.

Then, Merton said thirty-three words that have defined his teachings about interfaith relationships: "My dear brothers, we are already one. But we imagine that we are not. And what we have to recover is our original unity. What we have to be—is what we are."

Within a matter of days, Merton was gone. He never even published his own account of that stunning moment in Calcutta. It only exists because an aide sitting in the room thought to privately jot down some notes to save.

What a haunting moment! Merton making fun of his own collar, then revealing the deep awe he felt in that very foreign gathering. Perhaps for us, too, the luggage we carry—all the planning and preparation for our travels and the day-to-day anxiety about itineraries and connections—are what limits us and perhaps what may even prevent travel from making us better people.

But I stand with Merton in the potential that awaits us.

Taking ourselves away from what we know—having new experiences, eating unfamiliar foods, encountering new customs, meeting people who are unlike the people we know best, using the medical services in another country, taking trains and trams and buses instead of driving cars, discovering what it means to be in a minority, and making mistakes—these are some of the ways we learn and grow, if we are hoping to learn and grow.

4

Making Room for Those Who Cannot Travel

"No one truly knows a nation until one has been inside its jails."
Nelson Mandela, Long Walk to Freedom

The opposite of travel—the ability to move—is imprisonment.

By law, we take away the power to travel for many reasons: the general safety of our communities, punishment of offenders, perhaps an opportunity for rehabilitation, and, in many countries, to crush movements opposed to the regime that has power. Whatever our reasons today, the founders of the Abrahamic faiths have urged us to maintain a compassionate connection with prisoners.

Nelson Mandela was not the originator of this prophetic call to reexamine our prisons. Nearly three thousand years ago, Isaiah—a prophet honored to this day by Jews, Christians, and Muslims—declared that the measure of true justice in God's world included our concern for prisoners. It's hard to escape that prophet's provocative call, because the passage that opens the sixty-first chapter of Isaiah is the very one that Jesus chose to read aloud in his rather rocky return to his hometown of Nazareth, described in Luke 4. When he went into the synagogue on the Sabbath, under what must have been the skeptical gaze of his old neighbors, he read from the scroll of Isaiah:

> The Spirit of the Lord is upon me,
> because he has anointed me to bring good news to the poor.
> He has sent me to proclaim release to the captives
> And recovery of sight to the blind,
> To set free those who are oppressed,
> To proclaim the year of the Lord's favor.

Leaping ahead many centuries, that's one reason why prison ministry has become a pillar of the Reformation movement. By the time of John Wesley, in the mid-1700s, it became a central pillar of understanding what the word "parish" truly meant to restless new generations of Protestants. Throughout much of his life, Wesley personally made at least two visits a week to men, women, and children in Britain's notoriously deadly prisons. He was so rigorous about this that his many critics in that era taunted the Methodist movement for its love of these imprisoned outcasts. Wesley ignored the derision because he saw the prisoners he came to know as his parishioners. Many British prisons in that era, especially the private prisons, did not provide regular meals, clean clothing, or blankets—and, in some prisons, straw strewn across stone floors served as the collective bedding that caused inmates to pile together in their own filth and disease to run rampant. The need for regular visitation and community service was obvious to Wesley, both from his reading of the Bible, especially those passages in Isaiah and Luke, and from personal experience—his own father had been imprisoned for debts. At the same time, Wesley was also becoming a leading figure in the British movement toward the abolition of human slavery—and saw the plight of most prisoners in his day as similarly violating God's clear compassion for captives. Anyone who understood God's mighty acts in the Exodus, releasing slaves from Egypt, should at the very least understand the need for prison ministry.

And today? Many congregations nationwide hear about the troubling issue of mass incarceration, as nearly twelve million human beings around the world are imprisoned—nearly one-third of them jailed without any formal sentence in prisons that often are overcrowded, according to the latest United Nations global report on incarceration. And—right now—that dire situation for millions is colliding directly with a worldwide consensus, reached just after 2000, on the social determinants of health (SDOH). According to the World Health Organization (WHO), "The social determinants of health are the non-medical factors that influence health outcomes. They are the conditions in which people are born, grow, work, live, and age, and the wider set of forces and systems shaping the conditions of daily life." In the U.S., our own Centers for Disease Control has its own listing of SDOH and says this approach to public health should be the rallying cry for improving America's health care system by the year 2030. Every major U.S. health care agency is now involved in this effort, including gerontologists and Area Agencies on Aging.

As professionals crunched all that SDOH data to develop practical next steps, one central truth emerged: The chief threat to human health and longevity is isolation and exclusion—the inability to move around and have contact with others in the larger community. Or, as U.S. Surgeon General Dr. Vivek H. Murthy summed it up in his historic eighty-two-page report to the nation in 2023: "Our Epidemic of Loneliness and Isolation: The U.S. Surgeon General's Advisory on the Healing Effects of Social Connection and Community."

More than two hundred years before this public health consensus, John Wesley and other church leaders already understood that truth. They had claimed that mission as their own, including regular visitation of prisoners whom many of them regarded as members of their parishes. These pastors and lay leaders had taken this to heart as a divine message that they heard echoing down through the millennia from Isaiah and from the lips of Jesus himself.

So, it is not surprising that, as a first-year student at Princeton Theological Seminary, I found work in a prison. But not just any prison. I worked one day each week at Holmesburg Prison, a maximum-security prison on Torresdale Avenue, in the Holmesburg section of Philadelphia. This prison, I would soon learn, had a reputation within Philadelphia for its inhumanity and exploitation. I had never heard of it before, but then at that point in my life there was a great deal I had never heard of.

My job title was "student chaplain." I worked Wednesday afternoons and evenings, during the 1975-76 school year, on the C-2 block that mainly housed drug offenders—addicts who committed crimes either to buy drugs or while under the influence of those drugs.

If moving 750 miles from West Michigan to New Jersey was one of the biggest and most challenging moves of my life, then taking a job at Holmesburg Prison ranks as a close second. I tell the story here because I regard my experience as part of my setting out into a world I did not know. I struggle to call this job an adventure, but I never again saw a prison, anywhere in the world, without thinking of this experience. In that sense, it was lifechanging.

At the time, I did not think I was heading toward a career as a pastor. I was more interested in a career in editorial work or publishing because those had been areas of interest for me in college. I was aware of people in those professional fields who had started out with degrees from fine theological schools, so that's what I decided to do—with the hope of ending up like them.

My "field education," which is what the seminary called these one-day-a-week jobs, did not have to be church work. Most of my classmates hurried off on Sunday mornings to Presbyterian churches in New York, Philadelphia, and the Jersey Shore, while I stayed behind in my room to read the Sunday *New York Times*. I can see now that I missed out on some valuable experiences—but, for my field work, I wanted to get as far as I could from the neighborhood where I grew up in Grand Rapids.

Even so, Holmesburg Prison was a lot further than I expected to go.

A massive stone wall with guard towers surrounded the buildings where a few thousand inmates lived. The prison was built in 1896 and decommissioned in 1995. For decades, well before I had ever heard of the place, Holmesburg Prison was the site of unethical and often torturous medical experiments on inmates. These experiments were conducted by pharmaceutical companies and well-known universities, and they involved testing a wide range of drugs and chemicals on inmates, including dioxin, a component of Agent Orange. The inmates were often paid a small amount of money to participate in these experiments, but they were not told the risks involved. Most of the inmates at the time were Black men, many of them illiterate. Some of them were awaiting trial and hoping to earn enough to make bail. The walls of the prison, as it turned out, not only kept the inmates in, but the eyes of the public out. Only in 2022, years after the human rights abuses ended, and nearly thirty years after the prison closed, did the city of Philadelphia finally issue a formal apology.

In addition to the medical experiments, Holmesburg was known for its sometimes-brutal violence and overcrowding. The prison was often understaffed, and the guards were known to use excessive force against inmates. And so Holmesburg Prison became known as a place for rioting and unrest. I knew nothing of this history when I signed up for the job. What I learned from my supervisor, the chief of chaplains at the prison, was that in 1970 there had been a major outbreak of violence in the prison, with over a hundred guards and inmates injured, many seriously. My supervisor movingly described to me and the other student chaplains how he held the warden in his arms as the warden died from an assault by inmates.

Frank Rizzo, the police commissioner at the time and notorious future mayor of Philadelphia, blamed the violence on "politicized African Americans" who, he claimed, attacked white inmates and guards. Reform organizations and community groups pointed instead to overcrowding, the lack of meaningful activities for inmates, and abuse by guards as the underlying causes for the violence.

Each year, new groups of student chaplains were introduced to the prison as a new inmate might be introduced to it. We were booked and fingerprinted at a nearby police precinct, and then we were driven by prison bus through the gates. Once inside, we received an orientation from a prison official who sounded as though he had given this speech hundreds of times before. For dinner that night we joined inmates in the cafeteria and ate prison food. I no longer remember what we ate or whether it was any good. What I remember was looking around—wide-eyed—and taking in as much as I could. I had never experienced anything quite like it.

Strangely, I don't remember being afraid, though I probably should have been. Student chaplains were encouraged to wear clerical collars, so the inmates would know who we were and what we were doing there. But my clothes and haircut and much more identified me as someone who did not belong there. I stood out no matter where I went.

In my first month on the job, I remember being invited to play basketball with a group of inmates. My initial response was: "Sure." Because of my above-average height, however, I started getting most of the rebounds, and that must have irritated at least one of the inmates. After several rebounds I received an intentional elbow to my lower jaw that resulted in a split lip and a great deal of blood. A clear message had been sent and received. I should note that I experienced no other violence during my time at the prison, not even the suggestion of violence. Overall, I felt safe, and on C-2 block where I spent most of my time, the inmates were respectful and often curious.

Since I was the same age as most of the inmates, a few wondered about the personal life of a student chaplain. One inmate wondered if I was allowed to—he hesitated as he searched for the word—"fornicate." Then, once that inmate had asked the question, others leaned in to hear my answer. I said something about having a girlfriend back home, one I intended to marry someday, which was the truth—but the thought of a twenty-year-old man who wasn't allowed to "fornicate" seemed alien to them. In many ways I was a stranger to them, as they were strangers to me.

On Wednesdays, I would walk up and down the cell block, looking into each cell as I passed, making myself available to talk. The prison was never in lockdown during the time I was there, so every cell door was always open, and inmates would regularly invite me in. In those cases, we would sit on a bunk and talk, and I would be treated to photos of family members, girlfriends, and often very young children, sons and daughters. These were always touching, and in some cases heartbreaking, moments. The inmates were allowing me glimpses into their lives. They wanted me to know them as human beings, not as people who had been convicted of serious crimes. Most of them, though not all, told me that they were innocent and had been wrongfully accused.

Early on, before I learned that my role was to connect and listen and show empathy, I found myself wanting to "do something" for the inmates on C-2, to be an advocate, maybe to show them that I could use whatever clout I had on their behalf. One time an inmate told me about his interest in something, and the next week I brought him a book I had found on the subject. Another time I remember writing a letter to a judge on behalf of an inmate. He had apparently convinced me that his story was not being heard, so I went back to my dormitory room at the seminary and typed a letter to the judge in Philadelphia who was handling his case.

The judge never responded, but I remember talking at some length about the letter with my supervisor. I'm guessing that my supervisor had himself written many such letters over the years, because he didn't scold me or point out how little difference my letter was likely to make. What he helped me to see more clearly, however, was that I was there to care, not to advocate. I was there to recognize these men as human beings. Letters to judges were nice, occasionally important, but my willingness to look at photos and to listen was far more important. I look back on that conversation as one of the most profound lessons I would ever learn for my life as a church pastor. And I learned it in a prison.

I realized much later in my life that most of the inmates I met were on journeys of their own. I was not the only one who was far from home. Some of those men I came to know were on journeys of self-discovery, others were on journeys of rehabilitation and recovery from addiction, and still others were finding for the first time in their lives comfort and solace in the form of spirituality. As it turns out, we had much more in common than I realized at the time.

I never worked in a prison again, though I did occasionally return to prisons—whenever a church I served was engaged in some form of prison ministry. The cities where I lived changed over the years, but the prisons, I must say, always looked much the same. According to the Bureau of Justice Statistics, there were more than 1.2 million people incarcerated in the U.S. in 2022, the highest incarceration rate of any country in the world. More than eighty percent of pastors in the U.S. have visited a correctional facility, according to the Nashville-based LifeWay Research, but comparatively few churches have ministries for inmates or their families.

Nelson Mandella was right: Holmesburg Prison tells a story. And the story it tells about Philadelphia is a wretched story, but one that should be remembered.

Monuments and collective memories

Many years later, when I lived and worked in The Hague, during the 2022-2023 school year, I would pedal my bike to the Scheveningen Beach on a free afternoon. Always, on the way to the beach, I would pass a prison that locals referred to as the Oranjehotel, which I later learned was a tribute to those who were imprisoned there during World War II. The walls that surrounded the Oranjehotel were similar to, and nearly as forbidding as, those that surrounded Holmesburg Prison. No one had to explain to me what I was seeing as I pedaled by. I knew immediately what it was.

The Hague Penitentiary Institution, as it is officially known today, is still in use, and part of it—the part still known as the Oranjehotel—is a national monument. The prison was built in 1919 to house minor criminals. During World War II the prison was seized by the Nazis and renamed Polizeigefängnis ("police prison"). Those occupiers used it to detain more than 25,000 people for interrogation, most of whom went on to German prisons and concentration camps. At least 215 prisoners were executed at the Waalsdorpervlakte, the sand dunes opposite the prison.

Those who violated regulations imposed by the Nazi occupiers covered a broad social spectrum and came from all provinces in the Netherlands. Most were members of the Resistance, but prisoners also included Jews, Jehovah's Witnesses, and others. After the Nazis had been defeated, the prison population briefly changed to Dutch citizens who had collaborated with the Nazis, and those collaborators, I learned, were sometimes taken to the same sand dunes the German army used for executions and were shot there. The entire complex became a prison again soon after the liberation.

Today, individuals detained by the International Criminal Court in The Hague are also held at the prison, separated from the rest of the prison population, but in the same complex. The ICC was established in 2002 as a permanent tribunal to prosecute individuals for genocide, crimes against humanity, and war crimes. Detainees who are convicted are transferred outside the Netherlands to serve their sentences, but during their trials or while waiting for them to begin, they are housed at The Hague Penitentiary Institution.

One of the ICC judges, from Uganda, became a member of the church I was serving in The Hague, and it was my privilege to get to know her and to hear about her work. She once gave me a tour of the ICC and the courtroom where she presided along with other judges. She told me in vague terms about the nature of her work, and without thinking I said, "Oh, that sounds fascinating."

Without hesitating, she said, "It's heartbreaking."

And it was then that I realized how she spent her days—reading reports and viewing evidence about mass rapes, murders, and other atrocities around the world. Every time I pedaled my bike past the prison, I thought of the prison's history—and of my friend's heartbreaking work. Once again, a prison had taken me far from the suburban neighborhood of my childhood.

In 2011, I led a group of church members to South Africa. Our eventual destination was a church in the northeastern part of the country, in Acornhoek, near Kruger National Park. We had established ties with a church there and were planning to spend a weekend together to celebrate our connection. I had even been scheduled to preach for them on Sunday morning. Before getting there, however, we spent a few days looking around, exploring Cape Town, and taking a cable car to the top of Table Mountain.

Not on the itinerary, but of interest to a few members of our group, was Robben Island, a small island nearly eight miles (and a half-hour ferry ride) from Cape Town. Robben Island is best known as the site of the prison where Nelson Mandela was incarcerated for eighteen of the twenty-seven years he served behind bars as a political prisoner. As an island, the prison had no need for walls such as those that surround Holmesburg Prison, but the island and the prison buildings turned out to be forbidding in their own way, as all prisons tend to be.

When the Dutch first arrived at the Cape in 1652, they used the small island just offshore for grazing sheep and cattle. In 1806, when the British annexed the Cape, the island was briefly used as a whaling station. But in 1845 a colony of lepers was banished to the island, and they were soon joined by others—paupers, alcoholics, criminals, mentally ill patients, and more. In 1931, those living on the island were moved to the mainland, and the island briefly became a military base during World War II.

In 1961, however, the South African government began using the island as a prison—this time for political prisoners as well as convicted criminals. The prison became known for its harsh conditions and cruel treatment of prisoners. The daily work, which prisoners were forced to do, was breaking rocks into gravel. Prisoners from this period included three future presidents of South Africa—Nelson Mandela, Kgalema Motlanthe, and Jacob Zuma. The maximum-security prison for political prisoners was decommissioned in 1991, and the remaining prisoners from the medium-security prison were transferred off the island when the prison was closed permanently in 1996. Today the island is a South African National Heritage Site, as well as a UNESCO World Heritage Site.

After taking the ferry to the island, we were met at the dock by a guide who introduced himself as a former prisoner on the island. All of the guides, he explained, were former prisoners, and today they and their families live in the housing once occupied by their jailers. Like all visitors to the island, we were most interested in seeing the cell where Mandela lived, and like most visitors we stood silently outside that cell and looked in. We tried to imagine spending eighteen years of our lives in a space that small.

Our guide also showed us where the political prisoners spent their days—making gravel—but made a point of showing us where those prisoners would sit for breaks. It was there, he told us, that the African National Congress was formed and that a constitution was written for a post-apartheid South Africa. Mandela was eventually released, and apartheid was dismantled, but many of the dreams of those prisoners remain unrealized. South Africa is in many ways a country in transition, still coming to terms with its colonial past.

Once again, a prison tells the story of a country.

The last prison I want to mention is inside one of the lesser-known archeological sites in Jerusalem: the high priest Caiaphas' residence. It is located, according to tradition, on Mount Zion, the broad hill just south of the Old City's Armenian Quarter. When you stand on Mount Zion, you can see across the Kidron Valley, all the way to the Mount of Olives.

As always with sacred sites, there is some doubt as to whether the high priest's residence from the time of Jesus was actually located there. Nevertheless, because of the tradition attached to the site, a church has been built there—the Church of St. Peter in Gallicantu, a word derived from Latin that refers to the rooster's crow and the apostle Peter's three denials, all of which occurred in the courtyard of the high priest's residence.

When a set of underground caves was discovered at the site, the assumption was that this must have been where Jesus spent the night, the pit being a place of incarceration, a prison. Today, pilgrims to the Holy Land are often led to the place and allowed to climb down into the pit, where they are encouraged to read and reflect on the gospel story.

The pit where pilgrims are taken was more than likely a first century mikveh, or a place of ritual bathing for men and women, as required by the Torah. The mikveh seems to have been enlarged at some point and used as a cistern. The owner of the residence would certainly have been wealthy, as Caiaphas was, but there is no archeological evidence to suggest that the pit was once used as a prison. More than likely, early Christians wanted to believe that this was the place where Jesus spent the night, anticipating his crucifixion, and it became one of many such holy sites in and around Jerusalem.

I typically explain all of this to groups that visit, but without apology I also take time to read the gospel story, to reflect on that night, and to understand the feelings of a man who most certainly knew that his fate the next day would be death. To be imprisoned, as Jesus was, is to experience loneliness and dehumanization. Each time I visit, I think of all the men I have known who have been separated from their families, who were made to wear prison clothing, who were known by number not by name, and who wanted more than anything for someone to be with them and to recognize them as human beings.

Prisons have profoundly shaped the way I think about my work, but they have also shaped the way I think about the world I encountered after setting out from home.

5

A Protestant Passport to Pilgrimage

*"It's a dangerous business, Frodo, going out your door.
You step onto the road,
and if you don't keep your feet,
there's no knowing where you might be swept off to."*
J.R.R. Tolkien, The Lord of the Rings

Like millions of other Protestants around the world, I was more attracted to the spirit of pilgrimage through the writings of C.S. Lewis and his Catholic friend J.R.R. Tolkien than from any of our Protestant "forefathers."

Those forefathers were a rambunctious brotherhood who disagreed among themselves on many aspects of the Reformation—but they nevertheless agreed that the idea of "pilgrimage" was a dangerous Roman Catholic plot to reinforce the ills against which Martin Luther had railed in 1517 in his *Ninety-Five Theses*. Pilgrimage smacked of a religion of "acts," and not of "faith," these forefathers argued. Luther led this chorus of condemnation—driven by his strong belief in the surpassing importance of grace, as opposed to works, for our salvation. Nothing human beings do—no pilgrimage, no purchased indulgence, nothing—as he saw it, would earn them God's favor. Beyond the theological problems, as Luther saw them, pilgrimages were simply another component of clerical greed. He and the other Reformation fathers considered pilgrimages a huge waste of money that was flooding into the coffers of everyone involved in these pilgrimage routes—rather than going toward helping the truly needy families in the pilgrims' home communities.

Sound like a contemporary critique? It could very well be.

In the next few chapters, I invite you to pack up and join me in a couple of my own pilgrimages, which I plan to describe as a way of encouraging you to rethink your own assumptions about these practices. Have you made pilgrimages yourself? I will be encouraging you to tell your stories with friends—and to ponder how those pilgrimages may have transformed your life.

But, if you are Protestant like me, we must begin by admitting that we didn't get much encouragement from our Protestant forefathers. Of course, it was easy for this all-male chorus of theologians to slam pilgrimages because they were stepping into the global spotlight long after the European frenzy for Christian pilgrimages to Jerusalem had cooled considerably. The passion for organizing the Crusades to reclaim Jerusalem had reached its pinnacle well before 1300—and what passed for "crusades" in the centuries after that really amounted to little more than regional clashes between armies more intent on controlling real estate under religious banners than any authentic experience of holy sites.

Just to be clear, Luther never mentioned pilgrimages in his *Ninety-Five Theses*. His famous condemnation came several years later in 1520: "All pilgrimages should be stopped. There is no good in them: no commandment enjoins them; no obedience attaches to them. Rather do these pilgrimages give countless occasions to commit sin and to despise God's commandments."

That was the Reformation consensus, but there was a wide range of opinion within that verdict. The constantly on-the-move Erasmus, for example, fired a few verbal shots at pilgrimages, but he never regarded them as a major problem. John Calvin, perhaps because he also had traveled farther than Luther, also was less virulent in condemning the practice. Calvin generally argued that pilgrimage was part of Roman Catholic claptrap, but wasn't the worst thing that Rome was perpetrating. Among the Swiss leaders of the movement, Huldrych Zwingli was perhaps the most outspoken opponent of pilgrimages as part of what he regarded as the distracting baggage of spiritual practices designed to enrich church leaders.

To keep this record accurate: There were, indeed, Protestant pilgrimages to the Holy Land through the intervening centuries—and, perhaps ironically, some who published books about these pilgrimages were German, despite the Lutheran disdain for the practice. This seems to have been part of the growing German fascination with science, philosophy, anthropology, and theology that eventually produced a leading wave of biblical scholars who were intent on exploring the "Holy Land" with a Bible in one hand and archaeological tools in the other. The other Protestant group that fell in love with the idea, if not the historic practices, of pilgrimage were those generally known as Puritans. That included the seventeenth century John Bunyan whose *Pilgrim's Progress* was such an influential book that it eventually inspired responses by C.S. Lewis, J.R.R. Tolkien, and their other Inkling friends. Of course, Bunyan's book took "pilgrimage" to be a kind of metaphor for our spiritual and moral travels through life. Keep reading—and we'll discuss that as well.

Unfortunately, the Reformation rejection of pilgrimage wasn't merely a matter of historical trivia. Protestants paid a price. Their Reformation objections led to a complex and often troublesome Protestant history in relation to the "Holy Land." Those challenges started with the fact that leaders of the major Protestant denominations were AWOL at the ecumenical table of Christian leaders that formed during the later Ottoman Empire to help govern the holy sites in and around Jerusalem. To this day, pilgrims to the main Christian holy sites, such as the Church of the Holy Sepulchre, are told that the governance of those sacred places—the authority controlling those altars, icons, niches, and walkways—rests not with Israeli or Palestinian officials but with a 1757 Ottoman decree known as the "Status Quo." And the only Christians recognized as that centuries-old decree evolved through the centuries were Catholics, Greek Orthodox, Armenians, Syriac Orthodox, Coptic Christians, and Ethiopians. Not a Protestant among them.

That history has led to many odd quirks that Protestants discover as they explore the sites associated with Jesus' life. For example, while some Christian churches in the region claim to be nearly two millennia old, some of the oldest Lutheran parishes in the region date to just after World War II. Anglicans like to boast to Christian visitors that they have a comparatively longer history in the region, but pilgrims discover that Christ Church Jerusalem only dates to 1849. And that makes them relative newcomers in a neighborhood where their Armenian Christian neighbors in the Old City claim to have had a parish running as early as 300 CE.

In other words, if you are reading this book as a Protestant, our collective experience of Holy Land travels are ambivalent at best.

Stumbling toward the Holy Land

Our skeptical Protestant history explains why a trip to the Holy Land was not one of my main goals when I became a pastor—nor did it rank all that high among the thousands of Protestant clergy who began serving parishes in the 1950s, '60s, and '70s. According to *Christianity Today*, *Sojourners*, and other publications covering those trends, today's multibillion-dollar Jerusalem-bound Holy Land tours really didn't start booming until the '80s.

So, as with many other mainline pastors, the notion just did not occur to me early in my career. For someone who grew up listening to his grandmother's stories, getting ready for adventure, and then setting out for what was to be the adventure of a lifetime—moving to New Jersey—the next years of my life were remarkably unadventurous, cautious, and tentative. No one thought of me as much of a traveler. No one thought of me as much of a risk taker either.

Then, twenty years or so after getting that first passport to tour Europe with my parents, a man named John O'Melia called me one day and asked if we could meet and talk over lunch. John had been on the search committee that brought me to the First Presbyterian Church of Wheaton, Illinois, but a mentor once warned me that search committee members are often the first to be disappointed in the person they selected to be their new pastor. So, what I imagined during the call was that John and I would meet, and then he would give a rehearsed speech: "It isn't working out as we had hoped, Doug."

If John was disappointed in my work, however, he didn't mention it during our lunch that day. Instead, we ordered from the menu, and then, unexpectedly, he said, "It's time to take a trip."

I had no idea that John was going to suggest a trip to Israel over that lunch—along with the assumption that I was going to lead that trip.

"It's time," he said, as though this was obviously an expectation, even a rite of passage, for every pastor. To be clear, it's not.

I was surprised, then thrilled, and finally relieved. With that swirl of emotion, I naturally said: "Yes. What a wonderful idea!"

At that point in my career and family life, I couldn't imagine going anywhere, except maybe for a few days at a nice lake, preferably not too far from my work. Suddenly, someone was connecting world travel to my vocation, making this a natural and expected part of my job. What a gift! I immediately recalled that one of the best gifts my parents had ever given me was curiosity—the gift of wanting to go somewhere and see things and meet people.

Over the next few weeks, John and I interviewed representatives from several travel companies, got together once again over lunch to talk about the details of the trip, selected dates to be away, and finally began to advertise within the church membership. Planning a tour like this requires far more planning and decision-making than I had previously realized.

John and his wife, Marty, were well known in the church, so several of their friends signed up right away and paid their deposits. And then, even more came aboard—more, to be honest, than I had dared to expect. In the end, there would be thirty-three of us, including my wife and me, planning to visit Israel, to fly Alitalia from Chicago to Tel Aviv, with a stopover in Rome.

As the details piled up, the concept of this journey evolved. The brochure produced for the trip by our tour company—aptly named, I thought, "Imagine Tours & Travel"—described our itinerary as a "pilgrimage," which was a new word to me at the time. I thought we were taking a "trip," as John had put it. Now I was contemplating what a "pilgrimage" might mean for me and the people who were going to travel with me. Presbyterians, as I have explained, were not known for making pilgrimages.

My title, also provided by the tour company, would be "tour host." Israel required groups like ours to have a licensed guide, so my role was not to give lectures at every stop, which I'm not sure I could have given anyway, at least not on my first visit. What a "tour host" was expected to do would quickly become clear enough. I was to sit at the front of the bus, close to the guide and the driver, in case I was needed to make decisions for the group. But my role was also to look after group members and see to their needs. In addition, I often read relevant Bible stories when we stopped at significant historical sites, I offered to reaffirm baptisms in the Jordan River, and I preached a sermon on Sunday morning toward the end of our visit at the St. Andrew's Scots Presbyterian Church in Jerusalem. In other words, much like being a pastor, except farther from home.

As my thinking evolved, I quickly realized that this most certainly was not a vacation. It turned out to be an affable enough group, but hosting them was work: Spending nearly two weeks with church members, counting heads every time we returned to the bus, seeing to individual needs (one person required hospitalization in Jerusalem for a serious lung infection), and eating every meal with people who were not my immediate family.

At first, I began to think of this as a "study tour," which sounded appealing to me, as if announcing right up front, "Listen up, people; we're here to learn something!" As it turns out, something more than the desire to see something new and interesting would be required for a pilgrimage, though what that was I didn't know. The idea of pilgrimage was still coming into focus for me. At the very least, we were planning to explore the roots of our faith, to see where Jesus walked, to sail on the same lake where Jesus sailed, and even to visit the place where, according to the itinerary, Jesus spent the night before being handed over to the Roman governor.

As I discovered early in my first visit to Israel, no one is certain where Jesus did most of the things he is said to have done, including the exact location of the high priest Caiaphas' home with its underground prison cell. Even the exact location of Jesus' tomb, I discovered, remains a mystery, with at least two competing candidates. It was the Roman Emperor Constantine's mother, Helena, who identified many holy sites in Israel in the fourth century. She was a devout Christian who once spent several months both in Jerusalem and in what was known at the time as Judea. To her credit, she seems to have conducted extensive research and interviewed many residents. On the other hand, Helena seems to have exercised some imagination as well. When she named places along the Via Dolorosa, the path Jesus took to the cross, she arbitrarily decided where certain events took place (where Simon of Cyrene began to carry the cross, for example) and introduced a few other places not specifically mentioned in the biblical text (three separate places where Jesus fell while carrying the cross).

Beyond Jerusalem, she identified the spot where the multiplication of the "loaves and fishes" took place. She pointed to the exact place where Jesus stood when he gave his Sermon on the Mount. She marked where Mary was told that she would give birth to Jesus. She indicated where Joseph's carpentry shop had been, even though many scholars today believe Joseph was probably more of a stonemason than a carpenter, as we might think of that trade today. She identified the exact spot near Bethlehem where Jesus was born, the field where the shepherds were visited by the "heavenly host," and so on.

The accuracy of her findings has always been a matter of debate. I learned on my first visit to Israel to be skeptical of many, if not most, claims about holy sites, though stopping at each of these sites is nearly unavoidable since churches and shrines have been erected to commemorate whatever was supposed to have happened there. To make a pilgrimage to Israel, I soon learned, would mean more than seeing the exact place where Jesus said or did something. The words on the itinerary could be breathless about these holy sites, but I realized that I needed to find a larger story, a more important truth.

Even with the initial letdown I felt after learning about these holy sites, my first pilgrimage to Israel was wonderful—and in some unexpected ways, a lifechanging experience, for which I will always be grateful, mainly to John, the person who invited me to lunch one day. Because our trip was a pilgrimage and not a sightseeing tour, I offered more prayers than usual, I read often from my Bible at various stops along the way, and I led worship several times. Among other things, I learned that a pilgrimage is characterized by setting an intention for the experience (perhaps to feel a deeper connection to the biblical stories), to participate in spiritually significant rituals (such as reaffirming one's baptism in the

Jordan River), having a shared faith experience with other pilgrims, as well as taking time to reflect on one's own faith.

For reasons I no longer remember, perhaps because I was sitting at the front of the bus and thinking about the meaning of pilgrimage, I announced to the group one day, over the bus's PA system, that "Catholics don't own the copyright to pilgrimage. We can do it too." After a few days in Israel, I was ready to embrace pilgrimage as an important part of my life.

To me our pilgrimage became a kind of worthy adventure. And this first visit to Israel would be for me the first of many such pilgrimages.

On our first morning in Israel, after arriving at Ben Gurion Airport in Tel Aviv and staying overnight at a nearby hotel overlooking the Mediterranean Sea, my little group of pilgrims from Wheaton, Illinois, drove north and stopped at a chapel overlooking the Sea of Galilee, known locally as Lake Tiberias or Kinneret. I forget now which biblical story I read—my first such reading on the pilgrimage—but at some point while I was reading I began to cry. I cry often, so that's not surprising, but I almost never cry while leading worship. And so, on that first day my church members learned something about their pastor that they didn't know before, and I remember that they were looking at me intently in that moment.

Mostly, when I cry, it's not because of sadness, but rather because of something beautiful—in other words, because I have an overwhelming feeling of joy. As far I can tell, that's what happened on that first morning in Israel. To put it simply, I suddenly realized where I was. This body of water, which was plainly visible through the large windows of the chapel, was something I had heard about since I was a five-year-old in Sunday School listening to my white-haired teacher Mrs. Peterson tell me about it. So much had happened here, after all, either out on the water or close to the shore—the calling of the first disciples, storms, large catches of fish, even the report of Jesus walking on water. And now here I was. For a few seconds I had to stop reading and consider this moment in my life.

When I reflected on the experience later, I took it to be a holy moment. Earlier in my ministry I might have apologized for my tears before hurrying on with my reading, but at that moment I recognized what I was feeling and then kept going as soon as I could speak again. It occurred to me that the moment might have been partly the result of jet lag, having just flown the day before from Chicago to Tel Aviv, with a stop in Rome, a flight of more than 6,000 miles. But more than anything I was aware of how moving that moment was to me. It was in a way like so many firsts in my life—the first time seeing the Grand Canyon, say, or the first time seeing the Pacific Ocean and wanting to run fully clothed into the surf. But this moment at the Sea of Galilee was much more than any of those other first times because this time involved a deeply spiritual component. What made this pilgrimage different from all the sightseeing earlier in my life was the connection to my faith—all those stories about Jesus that my parents and good-hearted Sunday School teachers like Mrs. Peterson had read to me.

Despite that story, I do want to affirm here: Going to Israel and visiting holy sites is not especially important for being a Christian.

Or even for being a pastor, though I understand why some seminaries strongly encourage their students to make the trip before graduation. I suppose I would always have been a believer without ever having visited Israel and seeing the land for myself. Christianity, unlike Islam, has no travel requirements. But having been there—having walked, for example, from the Mount of Olives across the Kidron Valley to the Temple Mount in Jerusalem, a path Jesus himself walked more than once—all the stories I have heard over the years came alive and took on a significance that they never otherwise would have had.

No wonder I cried.

To offer another, brief example: Whenever I hear about Capernaum—the lovely village next to the Sea of Galilee where the disciple Peter lived, and which Jesus seems to have adopted as his hometown—I can now picture it in my mind's eye and marvel that Jesus was willing to leave it behind to set out for Jerusalem for the last time. Sometimes the reason people set out from places they love is to do the thing they must do.

Crossing borders

When American Christians visit Israel today, they are often surprised to learn that there are Christians living there and that they have been living there since, well, the time of Jesus. Today Christians in the Holy Land are a distinct minority, making up only five percent or so of the population. What is even more surprising to American Christians is that these Arab Christians have quite a different Christian culture. Most Christian visitors to the Holy Land choose not to worship with congregations in Israel, but those who do discover a style of worship characterized by ritual, liturgy, icons, and clergy with elaborate vestments. Most Christians in Israel are Orthodox and have been Orthodox since the time of the Byzantine Empire. Even the Melkite Catholic Church, one of the largest Arab Christian groups in Israel, still uses an Orthodox liturgy, even though it gives allegiance to the pope in Rome.

Seeing Orthodox clergy in their long cassocks and beards, wearing pectoral crosses and priestly stoles, American Christians are typically not sure what to make of them, even though their theological convictions are surprisingly similar. Ever since my first visit to the Holy Land, I have tried my best to introduce American pilgrims to their Christian siblings in Israel.

On later visits to Israel, with other church groups, I would change the itinerary slightly, maybe to keep things interesting for me. One time, for example, instead of flying into Tel Aviv, the group I was leading flew instead to Amman, Jordan, and spent a couple days there, including a day trip to Petra, a famous archeological site in the desert of southwestern Jordan, dating to about 300 BCE. Petra contains tombs and temples carved into pink sandstone cliffs, which is why it is sometimes called the "rose city." Several scenes from the movie *Indiana Jones and the Last Crusade* were filmed in Petra. Importantly, though, arriving in Jordan allowed my group to enter Israel by crossing the Jordan River, as Joshua and his people once entered the land. We entered that time at a place known as the Allenby Bridge, named after the British general Edmund Allenby, which evokes the land's colonial past. On the Jordanian side, not surprisingly, the bridge is known by another name—the King Hussein Bridge.

One time, on a "free day" in Jerusalem while leading still another trip, I rented a car with my nineteen-year-old nephew, and we drove nearly two hundred miles south from Jerusalem to Eilat, a busy Israeli resort town on the Red Sea. We left our car in a hotel parking lot and walked across the border to Egypt. Once on the Egyptian side, we hired a cab driven by a Bedouin driver to take us to St. Catherine's Monastery at the base of Mount Sinai. No one is sure where the Mount Sinai mentioned in the Book of Exodus is located—as always there are several candidates—but we visited the traditional site, knowing that tradition isn't always accurate.

About the time my nephew and I set out from Jerusalem in the rental car for Eilat, however, the U.S. Embassy in Tel Aviv issued a warning to all Americans to stay in their hotels for their safety. The reason? That night, in 1993, then-President Bill Clinton ordered the launch of twenty-three Tomahawk cruise missiles into Baghdad—in retaliation for the assassination attempt on George H.W. Bush, the former president, who at the time had been visiting Kuwait. No one knew how the Arab world would react to this attack.

As we drove along in the darkness of the Sinai Peninsula, after midnight, our cab came upon a roadblock set up by the Egyptian army. Our cab came to a stop, and our driver was ordered out of the car. We could hear our driver speaking with an army officer in Arabic, but we had no idea what they were talking about, only that the conversation was animated.

After finishing with our driver, the officer approached the cab and shined his flashlight into the backseat where we were sitting. In excellent English, he asked to see our passports. "Haven't you heard what happened tonight?" he asked.

We could honestly say: "No."

Sounding deeply annoyed, he explained to us exactly what had happened, and we quickly realized that we were in a perilous situation. I had felt responsible for my young nephew during the entire trip, but that sense of responsibility suddenly took on new meaning. In that moment I decided that I would exchange my life for his, if it came to that.

Finally, after a few long minutes of deciding what to do with us, the officer tossed our passports into the backseat and told us to "be careful." Our Bedouin driver hopped back into the driver's seat, and we set off again for Mount Sinai. We arrived at the mountain just before 2 a.m. and started our climb. (Due to summer heat, many pilgrims opt to climb the mountain at night.) We reached the top of the mountain by 4 a.m. and could see little, so we sat down and dozed and waited for the sun to rise over the Gulf of Aqaba, which was a stunning sight.

By the time the sun was finally over the horizon we were surprised to see at least two hundred other pilgrims at the top of the mountain. There was no sound, only the smell of burning incense coming from a small Orthodox church. In that moment I felt a wave of gratitude that we had survived the night. When we started a conversation with someone near us, we realized that we were speaking in hushed tones, as though the setting called for reverence. I forget now when we decided that we should stand up again and make our way down the mountain, where the driver and cab would be waiting for us.

Wading in the Jordan

On each of my visits to Israel, the tour group I was leading would stop at the Jordan River, and an opportunity would be offered to reaffirm the members' baptisms. Only one person, as I recall, has ever opted out of the experience in multiple visits to the area, and I don't remember the reason, if one was given. Typically, as the tour bus was approaching the site, I would explain to the group the meaning of baptism in our faith tradition. We don't re-baptize people, I would tell the group, but we are encouraged to remember and reaffirm our baptisms regularly. In the course of my work, I have known people who have experienced a deep spiritual renewal and who will ask to be re-baptized. In every case, I encouraged them instead to *reaffirm* their baptisms. More than once, I have used the words attributed to Martin Luther: "[Every time] you wash your face, remember your baptism."

Not everyone who reads this book will share this view of baptism and the ritual of reaffirming it, but because of my faith tradition I have encouraged this view over the years. And reaffirmations, at least in my experience, have been important and moving experiences in the lives of believers, one of the key elements of pilgrimage. Having the opportunity to reaffirm one's baptism in the Jordan River, where Jesus himself was baptized, makes for a strong memory.

No one is quite sure where Jesus was baptized. Many biblical scholars and archeologists are convinced that it most likely occurred on the Jordan side of the river, but tour groups do not typically drive over to another country for the experience. Instead, most groups stop at a lovely spot close to the Sea of Galilee, which is the water source for the river.

To be precise, the water source for the Sea of Galilee is further north—at Mount Herman—and the water flows south from there toward the Dead Sea. Today, the water volume has been significantly reduced from what it was at the time of Jesus, due largely to irrigation along the Jordan River, with the result that the Dead Sea is now a small fraction of the size it once was. The Book of Joshua tells a story about how the ancient Israelites miraculously cross the Jordan River into the Promised Land, making the crossing as astonishing as Moses' crossing of the Red Sea. But today, sadly, the Jordan River has been reduced to a trickle in many places.

As a result, many Christians today prefer to stop for the baptism ritual at Yardenit, a picturesque site along the Jordan, located very close to the southern end of the Sea of Galilee. This location has the advantage of allowing people to wade into the water and, if they choose, be immersed in it. Since the Presbyterians I have known over the years were more familiar with "sprinkling" than immersion, my tour groups would typically step into the river, one at a time, at an ankle-deep location, and then I would bend down, scoop up some water, and touch my wet hand to their foreheads. As I did this, I would sometimes look over at other tour groups at Yardenit and find myself a bit jealous about their full immersion experience, but our own experience was nevertheless deeply moving and memorable.

When I had reaffirmed everyone's baptism, my wife would often step back into the river, scoop up some water, and then, with her wet hand on my forehead, say, "Doug, remember your baptism, in the name of the Father, and of the Son, and of the Holy Spirit. Amen." Not only is baptism central to my identity as a person of faith, but I am grateful for each reminder I have had. I would get off the bus any time and do it all over again.

Pilgrimage, in my experience, has sometimes included frightening moments such as my encounter with an Egyptian army officer, but much more often moments of deep personal meaning.

6

'Go Into All the World'

> *"One's destination is never a place,
> but a new way of seeing things."*
> **Henry Miller, *Tropic of Cancer***

Pilgrimage is addictive.

Once we begin to explore the world through a spiritual lens, we discover a host of connections that continue to beckon us. We can see our journeys forming a vast tapestry—not entirely of our own making.

A year or so after my first pilgrimage to the Holy Land, my persistent friend John O'Melia suggested that we plan another trip, this time to Greece and Turkey. I did not need to be convinced.

Nearly everyone who made the first pilgrimage signed up for the second. Others, who heard glowing accounts about the earlier trip, also expressed an interest. In all, forty-three people decided to travel with us, which was within one or two seats of a sold-out bus. I worried that this next trip might not measure up to the high expectations. We used the same travel company and once again, without asking, they christened our journey a "pilgrimage" on the printed brochure. This time, according to the brochure's front page, we were going to walk "in the footsteps of Paul," the apostle of Jesus who traveled much of the Mediterranean world in the first century

CE with good news (or, as he called it, εὐαγγέλιον) for both Jews and Gentiles.

As an experienced "tour host," I knew better the second time what my role was, and I fully embraced it. I looked forward to my seat at the front of the bus and all the other responsibilities of leading church members to places described in the New Testament.

Much more sobering was the task of preparing a will before we left. It's not that my wife and I had a large estate to consider. Instead, we were encouraged by wise friends to designate a guardian for our young daughters, if for some reason we did not come back—a possibility that we had never seriously considered before. "Better for you to make this decision than the courts," they said, somewhat ominously. This was a new wrinkle in trip preparation—and not a welcome one. Stopping the mail is one thing; confronting the possibility of one's death is another.

With preparations complete, the group flew from O'Hare Airport in Chicago to the International Airport in Athens, and we were met by our Greek guide and bus driver. The entire trip covered hundreds of miles over the next two weeks, and much of the time was spent traveling by tour bus. Many people who go to Greece prefer to cruise the Aegean Sea and visit the lovely Greek islands, and I should mention that our group did take a cruise—but only to three islands and for less than a day. I suppose our little Greek islands cruise was for us like visiting an amusement park on the last day of a high school mission trip—in other words, not really part of the pilgrimage, but enjoyable and stunningly beautiful. My lasting impression of the trip years later, however, was not how beautiful the Greek islands are, but how much walking Paul did to fulfill his missionary calling. The bus rides from place to place were long, and I found myself imagining what it must have been like to cover those long distances on foot.

Early on, we visited the Acropolis, of course, and like most visitors to Greece we walked around the Parthenon. More important, we also stopped at nearby Mars Hill, known as the Areopagus, because, according to the Book of Acts, Paul once preached a sermon there to the people of Athens. Not everyone who heard the sermon that day was convinced by Paul's teaching because the story reports that "when they heard of the resurrection of the dead, some began to scoff."

As it turned out, "scoffing" was not the most serious challenge that Paul experienced during his missionary work. Over the years, he was shipwrecked, beaten, imprisoned, stoned, and once dragged outside a city and left for dead. But the learned men on Mars Hill—some of them, at least—were skeptical of a teaching involving the resurrection from the dead and said so. I, too, stood "in the midst of the Areopagus," as the story puts it, and read Paul's sermon found in Acts 17 to my group.

I remember thinking of the experience as one of the most thrilling things I had ever done—that is, until a few days later when I arrived in Ephesus (not far from the modern Turkish city of Kusadasi) and stood on the stage of the great Roman amphitheater. That structure, constructed entirely of marble, is almost perfectly preserved. It is more than 150 yards across and, in its heyday, could accommodate up to 24,000 spectators, without a need for amplifiers and speakers. To demonstrate the extraordinary acoustics, the group sat on those marble seats at some distance from me, while I stood on the stage and read the story of Paul's work in Ephesus, which seems to have ended in a riot and Paul's rapid departure from the city. I did not have to raise my voice. Remarkably, my group heard every word.

The ancient Greeks may be remembered for their philosophy and theater and even the Olympic Games, but the Romans, we discovered, were great architects and engineers. Examples of their building included not only amphitheaters and roads, but also aqueducts, which were used to bring fresh water to cities. Roman infrastructure, it seemed clear to us, had made possible the rapid growth of the Christian faith in the first century and beyond. Our understanding of the Christian faith grew—and, as often happens, our trip turned out to be as much a study tour as a pilgrimage.

We saw the places where Paul visited, and sometimes founded churches, including Corinth, Philippi, and Ephesus. We visited all seven churches mentioned in the Book of Revelation: Ephesus, Smyrna, Pergamum, Thyatira, Sardis, Philadelphia, and Laodicea. A few of these are now ruins within larger cities.

We even had a renewal of baptismal vows at Philippi, where one of Paul's followers—Lydia, a dealer in purple cloth, a person of remarkable status for the time—was baptized. That stop proved to be one of our most important stops, especially for one member of the group.

As we stepped out of the bus, I grabbed my Bible and prepared to read from Acts 16, where Lydia is briefly mentioned. After reading this story, I spoke to the group about Lydia, who happened to hear Paul preach one day. According to the story, "the Lord opened [Lydia's] heart to listen eagerly to what was said by Paul." And she apparently did listen eagerly too, because when Paul was finished, she and her entire household were baptized, the first recorded baptisms on the European continent. Some scholars believe that Lydia is remembered by name because she became a leader in the early church, one of several prominent women in the church's earliest days.

So there, in the shadow of a nearby Orthodox church, beside a small stream, members of my group, one by one, reaffirmed their baptismal vows, celebrating Lydia's conversion and remembering their own. Among those who stepped up to the small stream that day was Patricia Locke, a member of my Wheaton church. I spoke the words I always speak on these occasions: "Remember your baptism, in the name of the Father, and of the Son, and of the Holy Spirit"—while making the sign of the cross on her forehead with fingers moistened in the stream.

What I didn't see—mostly because of the large number of people wanting to participate in the ritual—was that after her reaffirmation Pat suddenly needed a place to sit down. She remembers that "something extraordinary" happened in that moment, though at the time she did not have the words to describe it. A few years later, she wrote, "All I knew was that God had staked a claim on me in a way I have never before experienced. I was overwhelmed with the sure knowledge, perhaps for the first time, that I was deeply loved. I sat on a stone bench and wept."

Pat, a single mother with two teenage children, decided that she had been called to ordination and ministry in a church. Not right away, but after many conversations and a process of discernment, she did indeed enroll at a nearby seminary and eventually was ordained in the Presbyterian Church. All these years later she vividly remembers that chilly morning, the light jackets we all were wearing, the sunny skies, and what happened to her.

As I mentioned, I never saw Pat look for a place to sit, and I didn't see members of my group going over and asking if she was okay. I missed all of that because of course I was busy with my duties. So much of my work, over the years, was about being busy in that same way, doing the seemingly mundane activities of ministry. The result is that I often don't notice until later, sometimes much later, what has happened. I was responsible for leading people in the sacraments, rites, and other rituals of the church, and then, years later, I would learn of the profound effect that they had.

These kinds of journeys cannot be neatly separated into distinct categories like "study tour" or "pilgrimage." In all travel, it seems, people can learn, experience wonder, and sometimes find their lives changed. In addition to Patricia Locke, I can think of several others who set out into the world and who were profoundly changed by what they encountered—so changed that they devoted the rest of their lives to some new venture, often in service to others.

Among those transformed by such travel was Susan Drinan—and, again, I was not fully aware of what was happening at the time. This happened during my first visit to the Holy Land, during a stop at the small village of I'billin in the Galilee region of Israel. This was the first time I heard Father Elias Chacour—Abuna—speak. I saw something in Abuna that day that I have come to see in Jesus whenever I read gospel accounts of his life—boldness and courage, with nothing more and nothing less than the conviction that he was doing God's work. I would like to think that Abuna became a role model for my own work.

What I did not fully realize right away was the lifechanging impact of this encounter on others in our group. Susan Drinan, who with her husband, Greg, was a member of the Wheaton church, also responded to Abuna's words—in her own way. She was moved by Abuna's descriptions of starting a school for Jews, Christians, and Muslims (and several Druze). The idea, as he put it, was "to learn peace on the desktops of children."

It was a such a simple but compelling vision that when Susan returned home to Wheaton, she encouraged our church to become an early supporter of an American group called "Pilgrims of I'billin." Its mission was "to support the Mar Elias Educational Institutions and other mission projects that foster a just peace in Israel and Palestine." Twenty-seven of the thirty-three church members who went on the trip signed on to become members. Soon after, Susan retired from her corporate position with GE and became a long-time board member and advocate for the school. She served for fourteen years as chair of the international council that oversaw the operations and financial matters of the school (and later a university in Nazareth, the first Arab university in Israel). More importantly she raised money, awareness, and support. Early on, at a single event, the Wheaton church raised $18,000 to fund a classroom at the growing school. (Enrollment had gone from two thousand at the beginning to more than 4,500.) Another event, not long after, raised more than $20,000 with a dinner and silent auction.

Within two years of the first visit to I'billin, Susan and Greg joined me and a group of church members who returned to the school during one very warm August to paint classrooms and plant olive trees. In all, Susan made a total of twenty-five return trips to Israel and led three pilgrimages of her own. Over the years, the Wheaton church held more fundraisers and similar events to raise money. Guest speakers—including Abuna himself—came to the church to talk about bringing peace to a land torn by war.

Shaping our vocations

Travel seems to have this potential to shape our vocations—our callings in life—whether we are comfortable identifying ourselves with any particular religious affiliation or not.

Mary Kingsley—now known as a pioneering nineteenth-century ethnographer and writer—was raised in a British family that was notable for its accomplishments in science and the literary arts. She longed for adventure and the intellectual life herself—a yearning that led her eventually to the heart of Africa at a time when most such travels were undertaken only by men. Her parents were not especially religious. As she set out on her own travels, she carried with her what we might describe today as an eclectic and inclusive faith in God that left her open to appreciating African cultures and traditions in ways that few British writers could in that era.

Throughout her journeys, Kingsley documented her experiences and became an advocate for indigenous rights. When I discovered her life and work, some years ago, I was especially taken with her because it was her father who first nurtured an adventurous spirit within her, similar in some ways to Dad's influence in my own life.

Kingsley once made a lifechanging trip to West Africa at age thirty when she heard that her father, who was traveling there at the time, had become gravely ill. It was that trip that sparked her passion for that region of the world and its people. Unlike most colonial writers of the time, Kingsley immersed herself in the culture of the region, documented the customs she observed, and studied the languages and traditions with both scientific and literary curiosity.

Kingsley's writing challenged colonial perspectives. Her best-known books are *Travels in West Africa* and *West African Studies*. She spoke out against exploitative colonial practices and urged respectful engagement with African cultures. Future generations of female explorers owe her a considerable debt—because many others followed her courageous example. Unfortunately, Kingsley died far too young at only thirty-seven in 1900. She contracted typhoid while working as a volunteer nurse treating Boer prisoners of war during what the British called the Second Boer War.

Seven years later, on a small family farm in Pennsylvania, Rachel Carson was born. I had known of Carson's work mainly as the author of the 1962 book *Silent Spring*. It was only later that I learned about how a voyage aboard the research vessel Theodore N. Gill ignited her passion for environmental conservation and led her to write the book that made her famous. Carson's interest in science had begun years earlier. She was a biology major in college and began her career with the U.S. Bureau of Fisheries. She had written the 1955 bestseller *The Sea Around Us*, which won a National Book Award. But getting on a research vessel and seeing for herself the effects of synthetic pesticides changed her life. Though Carson's *Silent Spring* was met with fierce opposition by chemical companies, her work was responsible in no small part for a reversal of national policy and a nationwide ban on DDT and other pesticides. Carson often was attacked for her lack of prestigious academic credentials, but what she had was an eloquent passion ignited by witnessing firsthand the destruction of natural habitats and biodiversity. She was never the same after setting out on that ship.

And then, although as far as I know they never crossed paths, there was her contemporary Jack Kerouac, who represented a very different strain of travel and discovery. Kerouac's cross-country road trips in the 1940s and '50s inspired the movement he liked to call the Beat Generation. He championed spontaneity, self-discovery, breaking free from social norms—and, in general, what some dubbed "ramblers' rights." In some ways, William Least Heat-Moon was a successor to Kerouac and his restless wandering and insatiable curiosity. Kerouac's adventures were a reminder that the destination is seldom more important than the journey itself.

Born in Lowell, Massachusetts, in 1922, by all accounts Kerouac dreamed from a young age about escaping. After serving in the U.S. Navy during World War II, Kerouac's wanderlust seemed to explode. He crisscrossed the U.S. on countless road trips with a thirst for new experiences and encounters. Like Heat-Moon, much of Kerouac's motivation was the people he met along the way. From New York City to the sprawling highways of the West Coast, Kerouac experienced a great deal and then—this was his gift—he was able to translate all of it into riveting prose. He often traveled by car, but he also hitchhiked, rode freight trains, and even sailed across the Atlantic. As he translated his adventures to prose, they became about so much more than physical journeys. He embraced spontaneity and improvisation. His writing seems to have been influenced by jazz. The book for which he is best known, *On the Road*, made famous his adventures with Neal Cassady and celebrated the Beat Generation's ideals. His other books—*Mexico City Blues* and *Desolation Angels*—display his ability to find adventure and insight in some unexpected places around the world.

While I struggle to call his experiences on the road "worthy adventures," there is no doubt that Kerouac's restless spirit inspired my own. His words provided a language for what I was feeling as a young man—and in that way he blessed me.

Finally, we can't list famous travelers whose journeys led to vocational transformations and not include Malcolm X. In fact, Malcolm made his pilgrimage to Mecca as part of his dramatic break with the Nation of Islam—the Black nationalist movement headed by Elijah Muhammad. In March 1964, he announced his departure from the Nation, whose teachings already were being criticized by many Black and Muslim leaders as diverging from Islam's central teachings about the unity of humanity.

Then, in April 1964, Malcolm made the pilgrimage that was a turning point in his spiritual life—confirming that the true teachings of Islam called for peacefully breaking down racial divisions. In his *Letter from Mecca*, he wrote: "Never have I witnessed such sincere hospitality and overwhelming spirit of true brotherhood as is practiced by people of all colors and races here in this ancient Holy Land, the home of Abraham, Muhammad, and all the other prophets of the Holy Scriptures."

On February 19, 1965, he was gunned down in New York City as he prepared to address a new Organization of Afro-American Unity, a Pan-African organization he had just founded in 1964. He was only thirty-nine, yet—much like Mary Kingsley—he died while living out the commitment to global service that travel had inspired within him.

7

Daring to Get Lost

"Personally, I like going places where I don't speak the language, don't know anybody, don't know my way around, and don't have any delusions that I'm in control. Disoriented, even frightened, I feel alive, awake in ways I never am at home. All of my senses suddenly come alert again and I can see, hear, and smell …"
Michael Mewshaw

Much like Malcolm X's experience in 1964, if we begin exploring our global community in an open spirit of pilgrimage—we discover:

Wow! There are a whole lot of pilgrims out there!

Depending on how long we can linger and observe the people around us, we may discover that we're not alone as one race, ethnicity, or even a single faith. For example, if we have the leisure to visit the Western Wall in Jerusalem over a series of days, we will see Catholic and Protestant pilgrims—and we also will encounter individual Jews and Jewish groups from around the world. Jews travel to their holy sites in Jerusalem either on their own or through a long list of programs. Since its founding in 1999, Birthright Israel alone has funded more than 850,000 free ten-day heritage tours of Israel for Jews eighteen to twenty-six years old—journeys that always include some reflective time at the Western Wall. Or, if we sit long enough around the Western Wall, we may see groups of Muslims who have traveled long distances for the experience of praying atop the Haram al-Sharif, one of the Islamic sacred sites on the Temple Mount.

Of course, most pilgrims don't have an opportunity to simply stand around a holy site like the Western Wall, day after day. Tour groups visit such sites once, stay for a while, and soon are whisked away to other sites. During these one-stop visitations, we are typically focused on our own itineraries, and perhaps the little flags carried by our tour guides—so we barely notice all the other pilgrims around us.

As I have explained, that's not my preferred mode of travel. In fact, getting lost in the little-known neighborhoods and byways off the beaten track is one of my greatest pleasures in travel. In Rome, plop me down in a narrow side street far from the Vatican or the Forum—and let me wend my way through the ancient apartment blocks, shops, cafes, little piazzas—and I'm lost in a heavenly reverie. I love feeling unmoored from the established patterns we are expected to follow.

And that's why I urge travelers: *Don't be afraid to get lost!*

I certainly didn't make up that bit of wisdom. In fact, like many of the questions and challenges I am posing in this book, that wisdom is thousands of years old. Every year, as they have for thousands of years, observant Jews mark the Three Pilgrimage Festivals. This is regarded as a commandment, but the ancient purpose behind those festivals was to remind people of the opening line of this book: "Travel is our origin story." In spring, the first two Jewish Pilgrimage Festivals are Passover and Shavuot, a harvest celebration that Christians remember by the alternative name, Pentecost. It's the reason Jesus' Jewish followers "gathered all together in one place" (Acts 2) on that spring day two thousand years ago, which became known as the birthday of the Christian church. In autumn, after the Jewish High Holy Days, there is a third Pilgrimage Festival, Sukkot. This is a beloved family tradition in which Jews are called to live as much as possible—including sharing meals and sometimes even sleeping overnight—in a temporary "hut" or "booth" called a *sukkah*. One of the most revered commands among the rules for building your family's *sukkah* is to thatch the roof with cut fronds or boughs laid out loosely enough that, after dinner, we can look up through gaps in our leafy ceiling to see the dark night sky and, on cloudless nights, lose ourselves in wonderment of the stars above.

The longer I research and experience pilgrimages, the more I realize: This calling to get spiritually lost in a journey may well be universal.

That's true even among the millions who now say they have no religious affiliation. In 2024, Pew Research summarized its latest in-depth study of unaffiliated Americans. Lumping these folks who decline to provide pollsters with a traditional religious label is not the same as saying they have no faith. In fact, Pew finds seventy percent of the unaffiliated believe in God or another higher power and half describe themselves as "spiritual." If you read that ninety-six-page Pew report, you will discover that all of us need to find new words and phrases to describe these timeless, universal impulses we share. That's also true for journalists and authors like me, wondering about questions like: Is the multiday Chinese New Year festival a public holiday, a religious observance, or a kind of family pilgrimage? This matters because that homecoming festival involves so many millions of people going home for a visit each year that it has become the largest annual human migration on Earth. The Chinese government prefers to see this as a cultural tradition; many Chinese see this as a deeper spiritual quest to reconnect with home and family.

How should governments categorize and control the annual Islamic *hajj*? Several million people meet the challenges of that journey each year—because making this pilgrimage once in one's lifetime is one of the five pillars of the faith for those who are healthy enough and can afford the journey. In 1964, Malcolm X needed financial help from his half sister Ella Little-Collins to afford the trip. And what should public policy say about women who want to make the pilgrimage? In recent years, a growing number of women have participated in the *hajj* and have been permitted to do so without a male guardian if they are traveling in a group of women. Among American officials monitoring world travel, gender is not an issue, but this is an issue in Saudi Arabia where pilgrimage visas are issued. Is the *hajj* only a pilgrimage? Or is it an opportunity for spiritual and perhaps gender awakening?

Hinduism also has a large number of important pilgrimage sites and holy cities. In Sanskrit, the central term for a pilgrimage place is *tirtha*, often a crossing place or a ford where one leaves the mundane world and crosses over into a more powerful and spiritual realm. The emphasis on cleansing from sin is similar in some ways to the Christian understanding of baptism. The term also points to the centrality of water, rivers, and bathing in Hindu spirituality. The largest cycle of such visits to sacred waters is Kumbh Mela, or "festival of the sacred pitcher." Following a complex calendar of sites—and both large and small festivals—Kumbh Mela is now widely regarded as the largest peaceful gathering of pilgrims in the world, with over 100 million participants on some occasions. However, until recent years, Kumbh Mela was largely unknown in the U.S. That's because American journalists and other media professionals were largely unaware of this complex series of rituals. Kumbh Mela simply did not look like any Western religious gathering. Indian journalists themselves have consciously produced more stories for Western audiences to remedy this misunderstanding.

What you've just read is only a quick survey of our complex spiritual landscape. Native Americans and other indigenous peoples around the world visit distant sacred sites; Buddhists meditate at places once associated with the founder of their faith; Jains and Zoroastrians have holy sites. And the list of pilgrimages goes on and on.

From Graceland to Burning Man and Thoreau to Dillard

Pilgrimage of course also has its secular counterparts. I was surprised to learn, for example, how many people visit Elvis Presley's home in Memphis, Tennessee, each year. (More than 600,000.) Given the quasi-religious devotion of Elvis' fans, maybe it's not entirely accurate to call this pilgrimage to Graceland a secular one. The Strawberry Fields monument in New York's Central Park is for many a similar kind of destination. It's a 2.5-acre site not far from where John Lennon was murdered, just outside The Dakota, the co-op apartment building where he once lived.

Perhaps a better example of a secular pilgrimage is the way Australians think about visiting the Gallipoli peninsula in Turkey. During World War I, Australians fought on the side of the British to capture Constantinople and force open the Dardanelles Strait. Though the attempt failed, and hundreds of lives were lost on both sides, the campaign is often considered to be the beginning of a national consciousness for Australia. After a long colonial history, the Commonwealth of Australia was established in 1901, but some say that the country's role in World War I created a new sense of national identity. Young Australians who visit Turkey today report that the battlefield tour is charged with pride and meaning, even lifechanging.

In many ways, the ultimate secular pilgrimage today is the Burning Man festival, an annual, weeklong event held in Nevada's Black Rock Desert. The tradition began in 1986 with an end-of-summer torching of a wooden figure on a public beach in San Francisco by a circle of the founders' friends. It moved to Black Rock Desert four years later and attendance swelled each year until the crowd peaked pre-COVID at a record of nearly 79,000. Organizers say that numbers now are bouncing back to pre-pandemic levels, although the 2024 festival was the first time that tickets were not sold out.

"Radical self-expression" is one of the key features, along with participatory art installations. Many participants remark about the extraordinary communal spirit they encounter. The experience is reportedly lifechanging for many. Certainly, Burning Man as well as other, similar pilgrimages reveal a deep longing for the spiritual, though perhaps "liminal" is the better word in this connection.

"Liminality" as a concept has taken its own long, winding pathway from mentions early in the twentieth century to a flowering of the concept in the '60s—and a number of alternative terms like "thin places" that have been proposed by other writers. In Latin, "limen" means threshold. Doorways, stairways, and hallways are examples of physical liminal places, while adolescence is in many ways a psychological one. Going away to school, graduation, getting married/divorced, and changes in career/retirement are also examples of psychological liminal places in our lives. People experience liminal places at several points in their lives. Liminal places can open us to new possibilities, and many people view their pilgrimage destinations as liminal places. Celtic writers, especially bestselling Christian author Philip Jenkins, have popularized a similar idea to describe places like the island of Iona off Scotland's western coast as closer to heaven in some indescribable way.

The American master who introduced liminal spaces to millions of readers is the Pulitzer Prize-winning author Annie Dillard, who has a powerful ability to choose words that frame unforgettable visions of these spaces. In 1974, she opened her Pulitzer-winning memoir, *Pilgrim at Tinker Creek*, with a chapter called "Heaven and Earth in Jest," which has the unforgettable image of a night-prowling cat jumping onto her through an open window near her bed in the middle of one night. The cat leaves bloody pawprints on her body from the cat's earlier nocturnal adventures. She wonders: What kind of struggle had occurred outside while she was dreaming? What was the source of this blood that now marked her body? "The sign on my body could have been an emblem or a stain, the keys to the kingdom or the mark of Cain." And this is how she describes the liminal experience of waking: "to mystery, rumors of death, beauty, violence." She calls these "morning matters, pictures you dream as the final wave heaves you up on the sand to the bright light and drying air."

Anyone who has read that opening chapter of *Tinker Creek* can never forget that cat and the mysterious bloody marks left by its paws. The book is based on Dillard's explorations outside Roanoke in Virginia's Blue Ridge Mountains—and yet these adventures now shared by millions of readers took place almost in her back yard. Tinker Creek was less than two miles from where she lived. It was her interior journey, however, that led her so far from home. The book touches on themes like faith, nature, and awareness, but—remarkably—the book also explores subjects like theodicy and the cruelty of the natural world.

The more Dillard looked, the more she saw.

At the time, Dillard was newly married, but she didn't think anyone would want to read a memoir by, as she puts it, a "Virginia housewife," so she left her domestic life out of the book and turned her surroundings into a wilderness that she felt compelled to explore and describe. The result is that she found spiritual meaning not by flying to a famous destination somewhere in the world, but by being intentional in observing the natural world near her home. Though she rejects the label of nature writer, the book is often compared in genre and narrative arc to Henry David Thoreau's *Walden*, which was also the subject of Dillard's master's thesis.

In a sense, Thoreau, like Dillard, was also a pilgrim. By making his home for two years, two months, and two days next to Walden Pond, he, too, set out on a journey of discovery, even though he was never very far from the village of Concord, Massachusetts. Thoreau simply found a quiet place to live, and there he took daily walks and reflected on what he saw—an outward journey with an inward purpose.

In this same category, I would include Cheryl Strayed and the memoir of her journey, titled *Wild: From Lost to Found on the Pacific Crest Trail*. Many people have walked the Pacific Crest Trail, though not many have found the same spiritual insight or had the same lifechanging experience that Strayed did. Part of the story, of course, is that Strayed walked alone, something that few women do. A fellow hiker, in fact, once called her "the only girl in the woods." Walking alone allowed Strayed to process much of her life to that point and find something within herself she didn't know she had. Much of her writing and reflection in *Wild* can be compared to Dillard and Thoreau.

In my reading of their work, all three are describing pilgrimages, even though the lengths of their travels varied so widely. Remember that the Latin origin of the term "pilgrimage" is "peregrinus," which suggests words like "foreigner" or "alien" or someone who has "come from afar." Dillard walked and observed in the woods near her home as a stranger or a foreigner to this realm, opening herself to a world she did not know, making observations, and exploring hunches. As she puts it, "I came to the creek not to fish or swim or even to look at it, but to find out what it said."

As it turns out, it said a lot.

8

So Many Roads!

> *"Even secular pilgrims on the Camino de Santiago speak of healing and wholeness, forgiveness and redemption, the miraculous and the inexplicable."*
>
> **Phil Cousineau, The Art of the Pilgrimage: The Seekers' Guide to Making Travel Sacred**

So, as we near the halfway point of our journey, I am reminding myself—and you as my friends accompanying me through these stories—of a central question: Have our pilgrimages made us better people?

To be honest, it may be too soon to answer that question. In fact, maybe we can *never* definitively answer that query. Perhaps part of the ever-accumulating wisdom of pilgrimage is that the journey never ends and our awareness of what came before us keeps changing even as we discover new horizons.

Case in point is Annie Dillard herself, who will turn eighty in the spring of 2025. Even though she is widely credited today as a prophet of "liminal" spaces, here's a curious fact: The word "liminal" never appears in *Tinker Creek*, even though countless essays, articles, and columns have been written about her memoir that suggest she had all but coined that term. In fact, there's a lot about Dillard's remarkable life that fans of her classic may have missed. In 1999—a point in time halfway between her life when she wrote *Tinker Creek* and today—she wrote a fresh "Afterword" for a new edition of her classic. Much like my own experience in writing this book you are reading, Dillard concluded that it was too soon to tell definitively whether *Tinker Creek* had made her a better person.

In fact, she ended that "Afterword" with a final sentence that, on balance, was a wry dismissal of the value of *Tinker Creek* in her life. What was that 1999 verdict? Dillard wrote that she was angry at teachers who forced students to read her book—so that "a generation of youth has grown up cursing my name."

I love the humble honesty of such a "last word" on the subject.

Except, that's far from the last word on *Tinker Creek*. Annie is still alive, if irascibly private. She greets the world online now by warning that she won't meet with strangers and doesn't answer letters. So, steer clear! She's still, even as she approaches eighty, pondering the value of her life. By way of explanation, she writes "I need to concentrate" on her personal website.

Then she flashes that wry wit again and adds: "Why? Beats me."

So, if you're like me and you can't quite answer the central questions of this book—then, don't feel guilty. I'm with Dillard. It takes a lifetime to answer such questions. The point I am trying to emphasize as we reach this halfway point in our adventure is this: Even though there are no guarantees, you've still got to get out there in the world and ask those questions.

We are not alone in this cautionary advice. No less a theologian than Augustine of Hippo, who has been described as the "patron saint of restless hearts," wrote compellingly about life as a pilgrimage toward God. He encourages Christians to "enjoy their earthly blessings in the manner of pilgrims," but warns against becoming "attached" to those things.

More recently, Martin Luther King Jr. used the language of pilgrimage to describe his own inner journey to nonviolence. In his book *Stride Toward Freedom: The Montgomery Story*, King writes, "Living through the actual experience of the protest, nonviolence became more than a method to which I gave intellectual assent; it became a commitment to a way of life."

And if my description of my sojourns in the Holy Lands hit a few ambivalent notes, please don't let me discourage you from setting out on what, for Christians, is the mother of all pilgrimages.

N.T. Wright, the Anglican New Testament scholar, led a group in the 1990s from his parish in England to the Holy Land. Wright's book *The Way of the Lord: Christian Pilgrimage Today* is both his account of that trip and a guide of sorts to those who attempt to lead their own groups. Not surprisingly, Wright is alert to the criticisms of the modern pilgrimage. He points out, for example, that a pilgrim earns no favor with God for making the trip. Beyond that, he even acknowledges that the real "holy land" is wherever believers happen to be.

In his slim volume, Wright takes us to the Jordan where Jesus was baptized, to the wilderness where Jesus found himself immediately after his baptism, to the mountain where Jesus' transfiguration took place, to Gethsemane the garden where Jesus prayed before his arrest, to the place of the cross, and finally to the empty tomb. He describes details of the land's contours, rocky soil, plant life, and even the weather and dry climate—all of which contribute to a believer's understanding of the gospel story.

But the most gripping part of Wright's account is his description of visiting the place where Jesus died, or Golgotha, the Aramaic word for "place of the skull." As Wright tells the story, he spent a considerable amount of time there, thinking and praying. And, alone with his thoughts, he reports that "in a way I still find it difficult to describe, all the pain of the world seemed to be gathered there." First, he thinks of the pain and anger of the Palestinian people he has been meeting and talking to. Then, he remembers the "paranoia and painful memories" of the Israelis whom he has also been meeting and talking to on this trip. And finally, he thinks of the Armenian Christians living in Jerusalem to this day who carry their own memories of genocide, an event in history made even worse by a certain silence that has often surrounded it—in deference, as some see it, to the modern state of Turkey.

As Wright describes his experience: "… so much pain; so many ugly memories; so much anger and frustration and bitterness and sheer human misery. And it was all somehow concentrated on that one spot," the place where, at least in a creedal sense, Jesus took on all the pain and suffering of the world. But even that is not the end of Wright's experience. All of that suffering somehow surfaced in him, as he puts it, "the hurts and pain of my own life." And this too "all seemed to be gathered together with clarity and force in that one place."

In all, Wright reports spending two to three hours in that place before, finally, leaving it behind and moving on. And when he does, he writes that "I emerged eventually into the bright sunlight, feeling as though I had been rinsed out spiritually and emotionally …" And it was then, he recognizes, that "I had become a pilgrim."

This has been my experience with pilgrimage too, and it is why I am drawn to it and spend so much time at it. But I must add a caution. These moments of heightened meaning are often brief moments in what is typically a long journey, filled with travel, conversation, shared meals, listening to lectures, and lots and lots of mundane activity. Still, those moments of heightened meaning—the two to three hours of contemplative prayer that Wright experienced—are the moments pilgrims usually remember and long to experience again.

The humbling paths of the Camino de Santiago

Here's another fascinating truth about pilgrimage in general—and Christian pilgrimage in particular: There are more well-worn pilgrimage roads around the world than any human could hope to walk in a lifetime! That's how I discovered the Camino de Santiago in northern Spain, a path that pilgrims have been walking for more than a thousand years—and why I was so drawn toward walking it alone.

There is more than one Camino path, so I should specify that I walked the most popular path, known as the Camino Frances. For many pilgrims, it begins on the French side of the Pyrenees, in the quaint medieval village of Saint Jean Pied de Port, and ends five hundred miles later in Santiago de Compostela, a university town in northwest Spain with a famous cathedral. Much of the walk is through relatively unpopulated areas, though the Camino Frances passes through many small villages and even a few cities like Pamplona, Logrono, Burgos, and Leon.

Pilgrims have been walking this route since at least the ninth century. Over time, an infrastructure of market towns, churches, hospitals, bridges, and marked trails was created to meet the needs of the medieval pilgrim. In recent years, the Camino has once again, improbably, seen a dramatic rise in popularity. Martin Sheen has widely promoted the idea by starring in the 2010 film, *The Way*, directed by his son Emilio Estevez.

Other popular Camino routes include the northern route or the Camino del Norte, which closely follows the northern coast of Spain. The Portuguese Camino typically begins in Lisbon, though many start closer to Santiago, in Porto, and the Portuguese Camino has both coastal and inland options. The truth is, there is an intricate web of paths that once linked all of Europe to northwest Spain.

By the fourth century CE, making a pilgrimage had become a frequent expression of Christian piety in Europe. Pilgrims sometimes walked as a form of repentance, but more often they walked without any purpose more specific than to feel closer to God. Sometimes the destination was important, other times not as much.

The cathedral at Santiago de Compostela, the end point of all the Camino paths, is reportedly where the remains of Saint James the Great, apostle of Jesus, are buried. According to tradition, James was the first apostle to visit the Iberian Peninsula. When he returned to Jerusalem, in 44 CE, he was martyred, and then according to legend his remains were taken back to Spain for burial. They lay there unmarked until the end of the eighth century, when Santiago de Compostela began to emerge, along with Rome and Jerusalem, as one of the great pilgrimage destinations of medieval Europe. By the thirteenth century CE, as many as 500,000 pilgrims traveled each year to Galicia, the province where Santiago de Compostela is located.

I first heard of the pilgrimage from a seminary classmate who went to Spain and Portugal each summer to walk segments of the Camino, but I never imagined that I would be able to do it until I retired and had the month or so that would be required to complete it. My Camino began well before I left for Spain with months of planning and training. Not every pilgrimage presents a serious physical challenge, but the Camino Frances certainly does. And so, I began to walk long distances nearly every day in preparation. I also thought carefully about the clothes and gear I would need. And I read others' accounts of the experience and planned as well as I could. Before setting out I thought I knew, more or less, what to expect. As with nearly every adventure in my life, I was right about some things, but wrong about much as well.

I had planned my arrival and departure but decided to allow the experience in between to unfold without much planning. I had no idea, for example, where I would stay each night, only that I would stop every evening and look for a pilgrim hostel (known locally as an *albergue*). My plan was to fly into Charles de Gaulle Airport in Paris and then travel south by train to Saint Jean Pied de Port. I gave myself thirty days for the walk which, in hindsight, was far too ambitious. Still, I had to choose a return date for my airline ticket, and I decided that I could walk, on average, more than seventeen miles each day. My overconfidence—perhaps the word "hubris" describes it better—and penchant for risk-taking turned out to be personal traits that I needed to explore along the way.

So, after my trans-Atlantic flight and the train ride, I stayed overnight in Saint Jean and planned to set out the following morning. Another pilgrim might have opted for a rest day to explore Saint Jean, but I didn't think of myself as just another pilgrim. Also, after months of anticipation, I was not about to spend a day window shopping. So, in the morning, I found the pilgrim office in Saint Jean to get my pilgrim passport stamped. Stamps are carefully checked at the end of the pilgrimage in Santiago de Compostela for pilgrims who wish to receive a certificate, or *compostela*. Two stamps per day from albergues, churches, city halls, post offices, and even some bars and restaurants are required as proof of the walk.

I also stopped at the post office in Saint Jean. I wanted to mail some clothes and travel items ahead to Santiago de Compostela rather than carry them in my backpack, which was already heavy enough. Unexpectedly, the post office did not open until 9 a.m., and by the time I sealed the box and paid the postage, I did not leave Saint Jean until late morning.

My plan was to walk nearly sixteen miles that first day, which would have been challenging enough, but what I had somehow forgotten was that this distance was almost entirely uphill. The climb to the top of the Pyrenees is nearly five thousand feet. I set out on the last day of February, confident that temperatures would be just right for a long walk, but temperatures vary considerably. The temperature on my first day soared to the mid-eighties, which might seem just fine—except that I was getting a late start, feeling jet lagged, carrying a heavy backpack, and making the highest one-day ascent of the entire Camino.

I soon became dehydrated. By late afternoon I was only three to four miles from the monastery in Roncesvalles, just across the Spanish border, where I had planned to spend the night. But I realized that I could not go on. I was near exhaustion. I would walk for twenty feet and then stop to lean on my hiking poles. I did that several times before realizing that I had nothing left. It never occurred to me that a man in his late sixties, carrying a heavy backpack up a mountain on a warm day, would not be able to push through.

With the sun going down, I had no choice but to consider my options, which rather quickly narrowed to one. I would have to stop and spend the night there, next to the path. And so, reluctantly, I spread my rain poncho on the ground, and I rolled out my sleeping bag on top of that. I had no food, no water, and no way of letting anyone know where I was. I did have a phone, with unlimited international calling, but I could only use it with Wi-Fi. And wherever I was, on the side of a mountain between France and Spain, there was no Wi-Fi.

Fear has not been a big part of my life, but there have been times when I was afraid—like that time after midnight in the Sinai Desert, with my nephew in the backseat of a taxi, while an Egyptian army officer decided what he was going to do with us. And now here I was, on another adventure, once again with an uncertain outcome and the very real possibility of danger. I had no idea what was in the forest where I would be spending the night. I figured that bears and other predators had been hunted to extinction, but I didn't know that for sure. And since I never camp, I had no idea what people do in the outdoors when they have no shelter. I crawled into my sleeping bag and promptly went to sleep. I woke a couple of times in the darkness, but each time went back to sleep. I woke for good around 6 a.m., rolled up my sleeping bag, repacked my backpack, and set out for Roncesvalles—not the first time in my life I was relieved to have survived the night. I stopped for breakfast in Roncesvalles, and then set out again—sobered, but still determined—for my second day of walking.

In literature, and especially in children's fairy tales, forests are often scary places, backdrops for being lost and the terror that often goes with that. Because the forest is full of unknowns, it can take on an almost supernatural dimension. And then, with a mix of the unknown and fear, growth and change can sometimes occur. I wasn't thinking about literature that night, but in the months and years since my pilgrimage, I have come to see that something important, even lifechanging, happened on the first night of my Camino. The problem was not with my training and gear; the problem, I now see, was in me. I can't do everything that I imagine myself doing. I can do a lot—and I don't give up easily—but I have limits. As a therapist once pointed out to me, "You can't always make the universe bend to your will." That first day and night on the Camino drove home that uncomfortable truth about myself.

I learned a great deal more along the way, though never in such a harrowing manner. Because I was walking early in the season (the peak of the Camino season is late summer), I walked alone for most of the first two weeks. Being alone on a path, somewhere in Spain, I started each day by singing, which had not been something I planned to do. I am no one's idea of a singer, but there I was, with no one for miles around, and I found myself singing aloud. I found that I knew the first verse to many, many hymns. And so, that's what I sang. I also prayed. I prayed a nearly identical prayer every morning, a prayer of thanksgiving for my life and for the lives of all the people who are close to me. Saying the names aloud was an unexpected thrill.

Those early days of solitude soon gave way to meeting and getting to know other pilgrims. For lots of reasons, most pilgrims start much closer to Santiago de Compostela than I did. The requirement to receive a compostela at the end is a walk of one hundred kilometers (or a little more than sixty miles). And so, the last week or so of my pilgrimage was quite crowded on the path and in the pilgrim hostels. As a result, I met people from all over the world—from Russia, Lithuania, Estonia, Ireland, Germany, the Netherlands, Austria, Canada, Korea, Japan, Chile, South Africa, and more. Every day, it seemed, I was encountering someone from a different culture with a different story. I stayed most nights in pilgrim hostels, and at dinnertime pilgrims talked and shared stories. We asked each other not only where we were from but also why we were doing this, the only time I my life, I think, when "why on Earth are you doing this?" was not an offensive question. I will never forget the stories.

The intention I set before starting out was gratitude. I was walking out of a sense of gratitude for my life, my forty years as a pastor, and the people I have known over the years. As it turned out, the pilgrims I met had far more interesting, and often compelling, intentions. And I quickly found myself shifting into a familiar role, one with which I have been comfortable throughout my life. I listened. I showed my interest. I expressed empathy. Some days I even thought of myself as a Camino chaplain, and I wondered if my real purpose had been to come along on this walk to be present for others.

Early on I met a man from Ireland who had lost his job and marriage to alcohol, and he told me he was walking with his father to sort things out, to start over. A young woman with cerebral palsy from Estonia was walking to prove something to herself and others. When I asked her what she did "back home," she told me that she owned an accounting firm. And suddenly I realized that I had expected to express pity, only to find a well of admiration. A Jesuit priest from Chile, with a PhD in biblical studies, was walking to take a break from his work of founding and leading a seminary in Siberia, of all places. A construction worker from Lithuania, who smoked at least a pack of cigarettes each day, was walking to find out if he really had a spiritual life. He suspected that he did, but he wanted to find out for sure. He also seemed happy to tell me about all the Lithuanian players in the NBA and how to pronounce their names. I met an author of children's books who lived in Germany, not far from Zürich, Switzerland, where I had lived for five years, and we talked at length about how beautiful Lake Constance is. A man from South Africa was the headmaster of a school and, as it turned out, knew a fair amount about wines, which was not a subject I knew much about. He also seemed glad to share what he knew.

The only American I can remember meeting was a man with diabetes, the variety known as "juvenile onset." With funding from an insulin manufacturer, he had once walked the entire perimeter of the United States, stopping along the way to give motivational talks at schools, service clubs, and retirement communities. He was walking the Camino, he said, with a similar purpose—to show what could be done with his disease. The list of people I came to know goes on. These people became what is often called a "Camino family," those who shared the experience with me.

Most of the people I met told me, by way of introduction, that they were not religious, that walking the Camino was most certainly not for them "some sort of Catholic thing." And yet, nearly every person I met was engaging in a spiritual exercise that dates back many centuries. Pilgrim Masses in village churches each night were a living legacy of this Catholic tradition, as were many of the signs and symbols along the way.

Near the end of the Camino, at the highest elevation along the way, nearly five thousand feet above sea level, stands a wooden pole, about fifteen feet in height, with a large iron cross at the top. The Cruz de Ferro is, for many, the highlight of the Camino. Some claim that the marker was erected by Charlemagne in the eighth century, but others say it appeared in the early 1500s to symbolize the struggles of the Camino. Pilgrims—those who do some reading about the pilgrimage before leaving home—are encouraged to take a stone from home and leave it at the foot of the Cruz de Ferro. The idea is that pilgrims leave behind a weight or burden as they make their way to Santiago de Compostela.

Not wanting to add any more weight to my backpack, I took with me, not a stone, but a small piece of driftwood from the shore along Lake Michigan where I live. And then, as with many thousands of pilgrims before me, I walked silently to the cross, left my "burden" there, prayed silently, and then kept going. Taking part in religious rituals has been a part of my life, so I knew what to do and what to expect from doing it. As with any ritual, I enjoy the feeling of taking part in something that many people before me have done. When I participate in a ritual, I recognize that I stand in a long line of believers who have been in this same place before me. What was moving on this particular day was seeing so many new friends, so many members of my Camino family, who claimed not to be religious, participate willingly, even eagerly, in the rituals. They also knew what to do. They welcomed the wonder and awe of the moment and participated fully. I came away convinced that, religious or not, there is within most people a longing for the spiritual, for the kind of meaning that ritual acts make possible.

I learned a great deal about myself, as I always do on a pilgrimage, and not everything I learned was easy or flattering. At some point, for example, as the number of pilgrims began to increase, I found myself feeling superior to those who had not started where I did—on the far side of the Pyrenees. I saw myself in those moments as the real pilgrim, the one who was doing it the right way, while the others were mere pretenders. I was also judgmental about those who paid a taxi driver a couple of euros to take their backpacks ahead to the village where they would be staying. Imagine the disgust I felt toward those who were making their pilgrimage by bicycle! I'm surprised I didn't curse and shake my fist as they pedaled by. I even heaped scorn on those who had clearly used a tour company to find lodging along the way, thereby avoiding the pilgrim hostels (with the inevitable nightly snoring in communal sleeping areas), getting a good night's sleep, and having a private bathroom. The locals call pilgrims "peregrinos," so naturally the people I walked with would refer to these others in what we thought was a clever, but derogatory, way. These pretenders who took various shortcuts to ease their journey were called "touregrinos."

What I had to remind myself is that there is no right or wrong way to make a pilgrimage. There are no rules, only a loose collection of customs. People walk the way they do (or they pedal their bikes) for their own reasons. They set out with their own intentions, just as I set out with mine. I was disappointed in myself but recognized that I have lived much of my life like this. I can be quick to pass judgment and slow to show grace. I enjoy feeling superior, and I am not proud of it. A pilgrimage like the Camino will reveal a person—the good and the bad. I came home chastened and a tiny bit more self-aware.

Some pilgrims arrive at Santiago de Compostela, have their photo taken in front of the famous cathedral, get their compostela from the pilgrim office, attend the pilgrim Mass at the cathedral with the gigantic swinging censor, the Botafumiero, a ritual which requires at least a half dozen attendants, and then—then the great journey is over. So used to getting up each day and setting out, many pilgrims often set out again, this time for Finisterre, the "end of the Earth," a fishing village on the Atlantic coast, a distance of fifty-one miles.

I surprised myself at the end by not needing to set out again. I had finished the historic pilgrimage and was glad to rest. Besides, I had only one day before my flight to the U.S. But dipping my toe in the Atlantic Ocean and sampling the seafood, for which the region is well known, was too great a temptation, and so this time I set out by bus, had lunch in Finisterre, and spent a few hours enjoying the sight of the ocean, with gratitude for everything I had seen and heard and experienced.

Like my first trip to Israel and the West Bank, pilgrimage had once again changed the way I looked at the world, my fellow human beings—and myself.

9

Is a Mission Trip a Pilgrimage?

"Reformation meant ... earnest regimentation of the conduct of life, which penetrated every sphere of domestic and public life to the degree possible."

Max Weber, The Protestant Ethic and the Spirit of Capitalism

Protestants may not have a corner on the spiritual practice of pilgrimage, but we do have a near monopoly on what have been called "short-term mission trips."

Estimates vary, depending on how that phrase is defined, but national studies show that between one and two million Americans, most of them self-identified Protestants, set out for a week or two each year under the banner of a "short-term mission trip." The "mission" of these millions of travelers typically is twofold: spreading the Gospel message and helping poor communities by shipping in resources like building materials or clinic supplies—and then providing the sweat equity to help repair homes, build schools, or run community programs. The exact balance of those two goals depends on the denomination.

You have undoubtedly seen magazine photos of Jimmy and Rosalynn Carter nailing shingles on the roof of a new home. Their beloved nonprofit, Habitat for Humanity, developed its own vocabulary to describe the groups working at Habitat's construction sites, but Millard and Linda Fuller's basic idea had its roots in Protestant mission trips as developed through the Disciples of Christ.

What I am clarifying here is that, in your congregation, nearly everyone knows what "mission trip" means. But there is hardly a more easily misunderstood term in the entire Christian lexicon. Billy Graham's 417 large-scale regional and global gatherings from 1947 to 2005 were mostly called "crusades," until he started calling them "missions" in the wake of the 9/11 terrorist attacks and a heightened sensitivity to interfaith relations. Those Billy Graham Missions—huge stadium events supported by regional small groups—were not what most mainline Protestants think of when they hear the term "missions."

Ask a Mormon to talk about "missions," and you will evoke one of the most cherished pillars of life in the Church of Jesus Christ of Latter-day Saints. For generations, Americans assumed that the LDS Church kept growing because of their formally dressed, bicycle-pedaling young missionaries. But the truth always was that a young Mormon's missionary year (sometimes longer) grew the church mainly by solidifying a resilient sense of the faith and convincing an exceptional number of young adults that they should not stray from their church. To this day, for example, Mitt Romney, former Massachusetts governor and Utah senator, proudly talks about the importance of his more than two years as a missionary in France, starting in 1966.

For Catholics, missions have technical definitions that most Protestants don't understand. For evangelicals, missions are evaluated in numbers of knees bent, heads bowed, and souls saved in a wide range of public events. For Pentecostals, world mission is a global call to expressions of the Holy Spirit. And, for many members of ancient Christian churches across Eastern Europe, the Middle East, Africa, and Asia, "missions" has become an unsavory word, often denoting American visitors showing up with paternalistic attitudes about how things should be done.

At the risk of simplifying a subject that has filled shelves of studies, most mainline Protestant churches think of "mission trips" as opportunities for practical, roll-up-your-sleeves faith in action combined with fun and fellowship among fellow "missionaries." And much like the research into Mormon missions, years of research show that these trips build more inside of us than in the communities where we are sent.

Here's one more truth about mission trips: They can be exhausting.

I returned home from my first mission trip looking forward to some well-earned vacation. The high school youth from my church had traveled out of state on a large bus one Sunday morning in early June to travel to a much poorer community. I suppose we could have found poor people closer to home, but we liked the idea of going someplace, being sent out into the world to do mission. Something about that, I suppose, sounded biblical—and a little like an adventure. We genuinely believed that we were setting out to demonstrate something about our Christian faith.

We gathered in the church parking lot, and after standing in a circle for prayer, we said goodbye to parents, boarded the bus, and set off for a day of driving, with adult leaders in the front of the bus and teenagers in the back—sleeping, talking, and listening to music. We arrived at the work camp a few hundred miles later and were assigned to classrooms at a local school: boys in one set of rooms, girls in another. The desks had been pushed to one side so that we could easily roll out our sleeping bags. After dinner and a program with other work campers from churches around the country, we went to sleep in anticipation of our first day of mission work.

My home repair skills are limited, so I was assigned that first year (and all succeeding years) to a painting crew. Our task for the week was to scrape and paint an old house, one that obviously needed more help than a coat of paint. Other groups, led by leaders who claimed more skills than I had, built wheelchair ramps, replaced roofs, made home repairs, and more. The organization that planned our work camp had already been in the community for a few weeks, finding residents who were willing to have a group of unskilled teens show up and work on their homes.

I remember the older couple who welcomed my painting crew on Monday morning. Mostly I was surprised by how willing they were to accept our help, even after getting a good look at us. Crew members ranged from fifteen to seventeen years of age. I was in my forties—and not exactly an experienced youth group leader. Most of my crew members had never had any kind of employment, and so they showed up for work most days looking as though they were dressed for a day at the beach.

In the evenings, back at the school, after showers and dinner, we usually found ourselves on the bleachers in the school gym, singing Christian praise music, watching skits written and performed by other campers, as well as hearing inspiring stories from the various work sites. The group from my church always sat together in the evenings, but during the day we were assigned randomly—presumably so that the teenagers from my church would get to know teenagers from other churches in other states.

Mostly, the week went smoothly. There were no injuries that I recall—either on that first trip or on any subsequent trip. The crew mostly stayed focused on their project. They even interacted with the homeowners, which always pleased me. They learned their names and asked questions about their lives. I was suspicious, of course, because we all knew that sitting and talking with the homeowners was easier than scraping paint. All in all, we were tired at the end of the week, and pleased with ourselves for finishing what we set out to do. We were told that unfinished projects would be completed by other volunteers in succeeding weeks, but I remember that we proudly assembled on the last day, a Friday, for a group photograph with the older couple in front of their newly painted house.

The bus ride home on Saturday involved a stop at an amusement park. We went to Cedar Point in Ohio, home to "the world's TALLEST and FASTEST triple-launch strata coaster," which I was happy to avoid. Looking back, I suspect that the youth from our church would have gone on the mission trip even without the amusement park visit, but we told them this was a reward for their hard work. My strongest memory about that last day was not the amusement park but handing over the teenagers at last to their parents—and no longer feeling the heavy weight of responsibility I had been carrying all week.

For more than a decade, I went along every year—always to a community much poorer than ours, sometimes to reservations (like the Red Lake Reservation in northern Minnesota and the Wind River Reservation in Wyoming) and once to inner city Minneapolis. My motivation, I confess, was less about mission and more about forming relationships with the youth at my church. And at that, I think, I mostly succeeded.

Our graduating high school seniors were invited each year to speak in Sunday morning worship and reflect on their years in the church's youth ministry. Nearly everyone who volunteered to speak mentioned the mission trips as the high point of their experience. This was hardly surprising since it was also the biggest event each year.

What I ask myself, all these years later, is whether our trips had any lasting effects. After all, the work sites where we put in all those hours would need more repairing and repainting in the years ahead. More concerning, we had little or no effect on the various causes of poverty in those communities—and may even have caused economic harm by taking business away from local contractors.

So, I think about those youth who are now adults in the middle of their lives, and I wonder: Did we establish a desire in any of them to work among the poor later in their lives? Did we create a connection between Christian faith and giving of oneself in service?

What have you found in your experience—and in your community?

If you explore posts on social media sites about short-term mission trips, you will find plenty of negative views. Under one Reddit post about "church mission trips," for example, I found 975 negative comments, most of them scathing in their perspective. One person wrote: "Nothing hurts more than seeing entitled white kids come, have a sheltered experience here while painting a wall or laying some bricks, go back to their home church, and tell everyone how by the grace of God they managed, and how thankful they are for all the blessings that God has given them." Another wrote more succinctly: "Keep your kid missionaries and send the money instead."

Should churches continue to put the time and effort and money into these trips?

In addition to the experiences within the U.S., I have also had experience with some of the more ambitious international mission trips that are also increasingly popular with congregations.

In fact, my first experiences with adult mission trips occurred soon after I became pastor of a church in Ann Arbor, Michigan. Before I arrived, that church had established "mission partnerships," as they came to be called, in the Philippines, Peru, Haiti, and the Galilee region of Israel. Church members were regularly leaving for other parts of the world—or else raising money to fund their trips. Given my love for adventure, I very much wanted to visit these various mission partners, and my church was eager for me to go along so that I would come home and talk about my experience. The idea was that I would be useful in promoting the various projects.

One of the first places I visited was the Philippines: Dumaguete City, to be exact, a coastal town southwest of Manila.

In 1999, as part of Habitat for Humanity's first-ever build in Asia, Jimmy and Rosalynn Carter led some eleven thousand volunteers (including nine thousand from the Philippines and more than a thousand from the U.S.) with the goal of building more than 250 homes, an ambitious number. The 250-house goal was not met in that year, so the church in Ann Arbor pledged to return each year until the goal was reached. Over the coming years, the church also established a dental clinic in the neighborhood, because of its many connections to the dental school at the University of Michigan, and did their best to encourage local dentists to provide care to the new residents.

The homes we built were not gifts. To qualify for ownership of one of these homes, people had to demonstrate that they had a job, would invest at least four hundred hours of sweat equity in the construction of their homes, and would set aside twenty percent of their earnings for interest-free loan repayments over a period of fifteen years. That, or something close to it, has been the Habitat model since its founding in 1976. During my visit I was able to walk along Jimmy Carter Street, as it came to be called, and talk to many of the residents. Among other things, I discovered a neighborhood of grateful people, some of whom eagerly invited me into their homes for conversation, dirty construction boots and all.

One of the critiques of international mission trips is that they perpetuate a colonial mentality or, more derisively, a "white savior complex." When Westerners travel to developing countries to help locals, there is a danger of reinforcing the notion that we, as visitors, are inherently superior to the people we are visiting. This can lead to paternalistic attitudes and a disparagement of local cultures. There is a basis for all these concerns. I take some comfort, though, that most volunteers for this particular effort, both at the beginning and over the years, came from the Philippines. Still, there we were, having spent thousands of dollars on airfare to get there. Our privilege was always evident.

On Sunday morning our group worshipped at nearby Silliman University Church which, along with Silliman University, was founded early in the twentieth century by Presbyterian missionaries. Today, the Western influence is still obvious, but both the church and the university are very much a local enterprise. Striking to me was both the size of the congregation and the number of youth and young adults in attendance.

I was also struck that when the preacher said something humorous, he always changed language from English to Tagalog. In other words, the punchline was always in a language I did not understand, even though the rest of the service was in English. When I asked the pastor about this later, over lunch, he explained that "English isn't funny," an observation that I have not forgotten.

Another memorable mission trip from the same church was to Peru. During much of the '80s, the Shining Path, both a political party and at times a violent guerilla group, was active in the central highlands of the country. Men were recruited to the guerilla force, and those who did not want to fight fled to the Amazon River region, leaving women and children in some areas to a precarious existence. Both Reformed and Presbyterian churches in Peru responded by establishing community centers where women and children could receive food, care, and job training.

The church I was serving established a relationship with one of the Presbyterian churches in Peru and sent mission teams each summer to assist in a community center near the small city of Huanta. I went with these teams for two consecutive summers. We lived in Huanta and hiked up a mountain each morning to reach the community center where we worked. On the way up and down the mountain each day, we passed a small Presbyterian church which always seemed incongruous to me in that remote location.

One morning, on the way to work, the elderly pastor of the church introduced himself and invited us inside. He told us about his long service to the church and his experience with the political violence over the previous decade. One Sunday morning during worship, he told us, soldiers from the Peruvian army entered the church and ordered the men outside. The soldiers were looking for members of the Shining Path hiding among the worshipers. The men, according to the pastor, were shot by soldiers outside the church.

The pastor of the church and I were photographed standing both at the pulpit of the church and then outside on the front steps. Our mission teams were never in danger, and the threat of the Shining Path subsided through the '90s, following the capture of its founder, but the trauma of the experience in the community was evident. The pastor seemed grateful for our presence—not so much for the work we did at the community center, which never seemed all that important, but for standing alongside a community of faith that had been ravaged by political violence. I remember going to an internet café one night and sending an email to my wife in which I said that I felt more of a call to be pastor of that small church near Huanta than the large, wealthy church in Ann Arbor. My email was an emotional response to the stories we had heard, though, and I never pursued full-time work at the church.

Our mission team visited Huanta every year over the national Independence Day, and so our team participated in the celebration by watching parades and speaking with many people who were not involved in the community center. I remember saying to someone standing near me during the parade that Peruvians seemed "very patriotic." The response, in English, was one I will not forget: "Yes, they love their country, but not their government." Every member of the team learned a great deal about Peru—its history, its culture, and its people.

After that first visit to Huanta, members of the team traveled back to Lima, but instead of flying home to the U.S. we flew to Cusco, and from there made our way to Machu Picchu. I doubt that I would ever have visited Machu Picchu if it had not been for the mission efforts of the church I was serving, so I am grateful for the opportunity. But I still wonder about rewarding ourselves for mission work by tacking on a sightseeing opportunity at the end. It reminded me of taking the youth to an amusement park as a reward for their week of work. Still, seeing Machu Picchu was a remarkable experience, one with all the awe and wonder I had come to expect from a lifetime of going places and seeing things. My takeaway was that the Peruvians we met were far prouder of their Incan ancestry than they were of their Spanish conquerors. They spoke of the conquest as a loss of civilization from which they have never recovered. I wondered if my team was not one more colonial conqueror.

The Ann Arbor church's relationship with Haiti was in some ways deeper and more profound. Within the church membership was a considerable number of University of Michigan faculty—nursing school, medical school, school of public health, and more. Before my arrival as pastor, the church entered into an agreement with the Episcopal church in Haiti to build a nursing school near its Sainte Croix Hospital in Leogane. The Ann Arbor church sent medical teams—not once, but several times each year, to work at the hospital and to provide medical clinics in rural areas. But the largest and most long-lasting effort was establishing a nursing school—the Faculte des Sciences Infirmieres de Leogane (FSIL), the only four-year nursing school in the country.

When a magnitude 2.6 earthquake struck Haiti in 2010, the epicenter was near Leogane, and so the nursing school, which had been designed to withstand earthquakes (as well as hurricanes), became a temporary hospital. I visited the school both before and after the quake, and I observed the difference it made in providing much-needed medical services to the local population.

As with previous trips, I had little to offer by way of needed skills (though I did learn to do intake interviews and take blood pressure readings for the rural medical clinics), so my role was mainly to observe, meet people, and then tell our story upon return to the U.S. I still feel a considerable amount of pride in our work. I still think that the motivations were admirable—and in some ways less problematic than for many such efforts. And yet, the concerns remain.

As for the main charges leveled against short-term mission trips, I consider the Ann Arbor church's experience to be an exception. Perhaps the most significant way in which these efforts were better than most was the cooperation with local agencies, churches, and (in the case of the Philippines) Silliman University.

Arguably the best—and least problematic—form of mission trips is the kind that churches undertake after a natural disaster. From the Presbyterian church in Fort Lauderdale, I once led a mission team to Moore, Oklahoma. Just a few weeks before we arrived, in summer of 2013, an F-5 category tornado touched down and destroyed an estimated 1,150 homes, causing around two billion dollars in property damage. Our team stayed in a local church. By the time we arrived, cots had been donated for volunteers, so we didn't sleep on the floor—but, like those youth mission trips, we ate our meals together, slept in Sunday School classrooms, and did our best to help in a massive cleanup effort. We met residents who were still in a state of shock at so much loss. Our only tourist visit was to a memorial near the Alfred P. Murrah Federal Building in Oklahoma City, where in 1995 a domestic terrorist, Timothy McVeigh, left a truck bomb which killed 168 people and injured 680 others. Hardly a reward for a week of work.

You're a part of this journey

Throughout this book, I have been raising questions both of myself and of you as my companions on this journey.

This chapter, midway through the book, lays out one of the thorniest issues under discussion in thousands of Protestant congregations nationwide. I hope that, if this conversation is unfolding in your congregation—or that if you care to raise these issues—you will begin as I have done in telling and listening to our collective stories. Hopefully, you will tell about, and hear about, a range of situations, conditions, and outcomes. Your goal is to encourage people to talk among themselves about their own community's mission trips—or plans for such trips. You want the readers to come through this chapter, prompted to tell their own stories and ask their own questions.

Throughout this chapter, I have avoided drawing sweeping conclusions about missions, except that the experiences and the goals vary widely across denominations and traditions. Based on your experience, what have mission trips meant in your own life—either as part of a "visiting" team or perhaps as a "visited" recipient of such aid at some point in your life?

As you remember your own stories of mission trips, I will leave you with a few questions:

One seems obvious. Who benefits most from these short-term mission trips? In my experience, the people who benefit most from these trips are the people who set out to do the work of mission. And, if that's the case, why not acknowledge that at the beginning? In fact, it might be best to plan for it, to make the most of it. If you are thinking about a short-term mission trip, ask yourself: How can we create an experience for each member of the group that will not only be memorable, but lifechanging? Training in cultural sensitivity, for example, will be especially appropriate when members of the mission team have little travel experience.

Specifically, I recommend a substantial amount of preparation before making the trip to understand the culture to be visited and perhaps even the language where the work will take place. Group members need to visit with the intent to learn from rather than to impose their values on the people they visit.

And then, while on the trip, it is important to engage with the people and culture of the place being visited. On one of the high school mission trips I mentioned—to the Red Lake Indian Reservation in Minnesota—I remember sitting in the local high school's gymnasium and witnessing a drum circle performed by members of the Ojibwe tribe. A member of the tribal council then explained to us what we were listening to and why it was important to them. I remember also that he told us about his culture's strong tradition of respecting their elders. I have long forgotten the exact nature of the work we did that week, but I remember what I learned that night while sitting in those bleachers and still feel grateful for it. Members of the Red Lake Indian Reservation had not only welcomed us to their land but had explained to us some of their most important values. In hindsight, of course, we could have gone even deeper, but for many of us the experience was the first of its kind.

Another question: Is this mission trip we are planning a "one and done" kind of experience, or is there a desire for a longer, deeper relationship?

The mission trips I continue to feel most proud of, not surprisingly, are those that involved an ongoing relationship—in other words, not a "one and done" visit, which is too often how mission trips feel, but instead, a mutuality or, even better, a partnership that involved individuals or groups moving in both directions. I remember, for example, welcoming Hilda Alcindor, the dean of the nursing school in Leogane, Haiti, to a church in Florida where

I was serving at the time. Her visit to my congregation in the U.S. made our relationship seem more like one of collaboration and less like one of dependence. After being a guest in her home in Leogane, I was able to welcome her to my home and offer to her the same hospitality I had experienced. I could honestly say to church members when I introduced Hilda, "I want you to meet a friend of mine." And so, another question to ask before setting out is how to cultivate that sense of mutuality, partnership, and collaboration from the beginning of the relationship.

Since visiting mission teams sometimes take work away from local contractors, an important question to ask concerns the impact of mission trips on the local economy and local providers. Establishing a dental clinic in Dumaguete City, the Philippines, was certainly a generous and important gift to the newly built Habitat for Humanity neighborhood, but the clinic's long-term success depended on the willingness of local dentists to own both the clinic and its mission. I commend the dentists who visited Dumaguete, not only because of the hours of dental care they provided, but for the creative ways they reached out to dentists in the Philippines and the partnerships they cultivated. As I recall, the local dentists were more than a little skeptical of our project at the beginning, but slowly came to see the new neighborhood as a way to grow their practices and to foster dental health and hygiene in the area.

Related, but no less important, is asking where materials used in the mission effort will be purchased. Buying local may be one way to make mission trips beneficial to the local economy.

Then, though this is by no means a complete list of questions, there is the matter of contributing to a "mission tourism" industry. In other words, mission trips have a way of becoming still another form of adventure travel. Visiting Machu Picchu at the end of a mission trip to Peru, for example, might be fun and exciting, but what is the message to the local partners, the churches who extended the invitation to visit and work? Is it necessary to reward short-term mission volunteers with a visit to an amusement park at the end?

Finally, and this is no less important than the previous questions, how do we talk about our experience when we get home? Mission trip leaders might be able to provide some helpful coaching to participants as the experience concludes. Reporting to one's congregation, for example, that a mission trip experience "made me appreciate how much God has blessed me with material things [after seeing how deprived other people are]" might not be the most profound takeaway. It might be true, of course, that mission trips cultivate a sense of gratitude, but perhaps mission trip participants could be led to see another level of meaning in what they did, another way to understand gratitude.

10

Revisiting Babel

"Amazed and astonished, they asked, 'Are not all these who are speaking Galileans? And how is it that we hear, each of us, in our own native language? Parthians, Medes, Elamites, and residents of Mesopotamia, Judea and Cappadocia, Pontus and Asia, Phrygia and Pamphylia, Egypt and the parts of Libya belonging to Cyrene, and visitors from Rome, both Jews and proselytes, Cretans and Arabs—in our own languages we hear them speaking about God's deeds of power.'"
Acts 2:7-11, NRSVue

If Protestants love mission trips, they are even more famous for insisting that the Bible be provided to people around the world in their own languages. John Wycliffe is celebrated as a precursor to the Protestant movement for his translation of the Bible into Middle English more than a century before Luther's *Ninety-five Theses*. Several early Protestant heroes had to stand their ground on charges of heresy simply for translating all or portions of the Bible.

That passion was born with what Christians like to call the birthday of the church—Pentecost. As I noted previously, that is one of the three traditional Jewish Pilgrimage Festivals, also known as Shavuot, and the story in Acts 2 of the "rush of a violent wind" that passed among them was all about bursting open the floodgates of the early church—through language. Pentecost sermons today are preached describing how the bewildered followers of Jesus seemed to be speaking all at once in different languages—so loudly and in such a cacophony that Acts tells us the crowd jeered and decided that these Jesus followers must be drunk. Perhaps because verses 9-11 are so challenging for lay readers to get through on a Sunday morning, congregations rarely hear the rest of the story: Suddenly, these disciples, with their limited education, were able to speak the common languages of dozens of migrants in the region from all over the known world. Yes, they were "speaking in tongues," but this arguably wasn't the same as "glossolalia," which is a cultural and spiritual chasm separating mainline church members from Pentecostals to this day.

The truth is: From the first day of the church, the Spirit moved church leaders to speak in other languages. And that is why, to this day, millions of dollars of donations continue to pour into evangelical nonprofit groups still translating the Bible for scores of tiny language groups around the planet.

The first language I attempted to learn (after English) was Latin. I was in high school at the time, and students at my school were required to choose a language. I think the other options were Spanish, French, and German. I am no longer sure why I chose Latin, except that it seemed impressive to me at the time. My parents had no preference and saw no advantage in learning one language over another because everyone we knew spoke only English. I suppose they, like the parents of my classmates, wondered when we would ever be able to put this knowledge to a practical use.

Of course, no one speaks Latin anymore, except in traditional celebrations of the Catholic Mass, so I had no idea what use Latin would serve. As it turned out, the unexpectedly happy outcome of learning Latin was that I understood the basics of English grammar for the first time. I had never quite grasped the relationship, for example, between subjects, verbs, and direct (or indirect) objects, until Latin made all that clear to me.

I even continued with Latin during my first year of college—mainly to fulfill the language requirement in my liberal arts degree.

And then, almost as abruptly as I started, I was finished with language-learning forever. And to be honest, I was not at all sad about it. Soon after turning sixty, however, living in a village near Zürich, Switzerland, I found myself once again in a language class, this time to learn German. Not *Schwiizerdürsch*, the Swiss-German spoken by people in the north central part of Switzerland, but *Hochdeutsch*, the standard German spoken by as many as ninety-five million people around the world.

If I had wanted to become a fluent German speaker, I should have started before I was ten years old, which seems to be the best time in life to learn a language. But I didn't know that one day I would be living and working in a German-speaking part of the world, in a country where a work permit requires proficiency in the local language.

Every Tuesday evening, during that first year, I found myself in a small classroom, in the village language school, with a young schoolteacher and two or three other beginner German students like me. The teacher, who spoke excellent English, used only German during classes. She always spoke clearly and used simple language, but she was nevertheless speaking a language none of us knew. The strategy made sense, of course. How else were we to get used to the sound and rhythms of the German language?

In addition to language classes, I often sat with other expats at lunch time, and our agreement for the hour was that we would speak and respond to each other only in German. We took turns introducing ourselves—"*Wie heißt du?*" (What is your name?)

"*Ich heiße Doug!*"

"*Woher kommst du?*" (Where are you from?)

"*Ich komme aus den USA!*"

Generally, the experience was fun and filled with laughter. I quickly learned that one reason children learn language more quickly is that they aren't afraid to make mistakes. Adults, on the other hand, tend to speak self-consciously and are often embarrassed by even the smallest grammatical mistake. So, in language groups with expats, we made lots of mistakes and enjoyed ourselves in the process.

Beyond the classes and the lunchtime language groups, I read a daily German-language newspaper and on my train ride each day to Zürich listened to German-language podcasts produced for beginners like me. In my spare time, I even made use of language apps like Duolingo and Babbel, though I discovered early on that the value of these apps was mostly supplemental to other ways of learning. (Learning words and phrases—like "good morning" and "thank you"—before visiting another country is certainly commendable, but my experience is that full immersion is the only effective method to master a new language.)

The truth is, I heard German all around me—every single day. In the grocery store or the pharmacy, a clerk might say, "*Kann ich Ihnen helfen?*"

And then, seeing my puzzled expression, the clerk would invariably switch to English—"May I help you, sir?"

This happened more times than I can count and always produced some embarrassment. I don't like to feel so helpless. However, asking for help when traveling to other parts of the world is, I have discovered, mostly a good thing. It puts the traveler or newcomer in the position of depending on the kindness of the host. And that tends to produce humility, though of course not always. The striking thing for me about traveling in Europe is how many people speak not only English, but two or three other languages, as well. This is especially true among younger people. Some of the older people in our Swiss apartment building were not English speakers, and our conversations were sometimes difficult and occasionally humorous, usually involving lots of gestures. Younger people, we were told, learned English out of necessity, because it is one of the most widely used languages in the world. It is the language of international business, for example, and to a surprising extent it is also the language of academics. The two major universities in Zürich—the Federal Institute of Technology Zürich (ETH) and the University of Zürich—both offered classes almost exclusively in English.

Whenever I would express embarrassment at not being able to speak the language of my host, I would invariably hear the explanation that "it really isn't necessary for you." Which is true enough. At a practical level, there is no need for Americans to learn a language other than English, and as a result few of us do. However, each time this conversation happened, I realized that Americans are virtually alone in the world in expecting others to speak our language. What my years of living in Europe taught me, among other things, is that Americans might occasionally learn a few things from Europeans.

In his book *Reaching Out: The Three Movements of the Spiritual Life*, Henri Nouwen explains that, in our interactions with others, there is often an undercurrent of fear, suspicion, prejudice, defensiveness, and self-absorption. And importantly, this undercurrent prevents us from genuine connection and intimacy with others, an important step in getting to know other cultures—and essential for curiosity. So, for example, to move from hostility to hospitality (one of the three spiritual movements that Nouwen identifies) requires a conscious effort and considerable self-awareness. It requires, as he puts it, a deep desire to encounter and celebrate the humanity of others.

In my own travels, pilgrimages, mission trips, and living abroad, I have not experienced "hostility," as most people would define that word—in fact, just the opposite. But I have recognized in myself some reticence, even distrust, when I am with people who are strangers to me. I am nearly always curious about them, of course, but I am nevertheless aware of some fear on my part. I find people from other cultures harder to know than the people I knew back in Michigan, for example. I had years of living there to observe and parse the smallest nuances of language and facial expressions, but when traveling, that confident way of interacting has almost always been absent. And so, I found that I had to be deliberate and attentive. I had to make a conscious effort to understand. I had to ask questions of strangers, thereby putting myself, as I mentioned, in a more vulnerable position.

I have come to see language learning as part of the movement from hostility to hospitality. David I. Smith, a professor at Calvin University, has written persuasively about language learning as a critical component of hospitality, of creating a "free, friendly space" with strangers, shifting the focus, as he puts it, "from mastery to encounter." Smith started his career teaching French, German, and Russian in public secondary schools in the U.K. He now works with Christian college students and teaches them that learning from the stranger is more important to Christian discipleship than imparting our knowledge and wisdom to them.

In nearly every pastoral encounter I had in my work abroad, I found myself asking, "What is it about this person's background and culture that is leading her or him to speak and act in this way?" Frankly, it can be exhausting work. The habits and attitudes I understood and took for granted in my U.S. churches were not easily transferred to my new pastoral setting. I found that meetings lasted longer than those in the U.S. and were occasionally exasperating, but always the intent was to discover what the other person meant to say. I wish I could say that my mastery of German always helped me to understand the people I met, but occasionally a word or phrase took on new meaning. Occasionally I would have an insight into a conflicted situation because of a concept I had learned in my weekly language class.

More than anything, what I take away from Smith's work, especially his book *Learning from the Stranger: Christian Faith and Cultural Diversity*, is his notion that "learning from the stranger … is a necessary component of genuinely loving one's neighbor."

Smith is not alone in maintaining that language learning is an act of hospitality and a way to overcome cultural barriers. Many writers have made a similar point. Henry Pratt, who teaches linguistics at the University of Kansas, has written in an essay titled "Hospitality and the Ethics of Crossing Borders" that language learning involves "opening oneself up to the Other and their culture." He emphasizes the critical importance of humility and respect and suggests that the language learning can be a way to challenge ethnocentrism and promote intercultural understanding.

Asif Agha, a linguist at the University of California at Los Angeles, argues that language learning can be a form of "linguistic citizenship" and that it can be used to challenge power imbalances and promote social justice.

In his essay "Learning Another Language as a Form of Ethical Engagement," Michael Cronin, an Irish academic, argues that language learning is nothing less than an ethical imperative, because it allows us to engage with others on their own terms and on their own ground. Cronin maintains that language learning can help us to develop empathy and understanding for different cultures.

The French philosopher Jacques Derrida, in an essay titled "Hospitality and the Ethics of Communication," offers a somewhat theoretical exploration of the relationship between hospitality and communication. Derrida writes that true hospitality requires an openness to the other that is not limited by language. However, he also acknowledges that language is an essential part of the hospitality experience, and that learning another language can be a way of showing respect and openness to the other.

Polyglot and translator Siri Hustved, in her book *A Plea for Babel*, rather eloquently argues that language learning is not just about acquiring a new skill but rather about "becoming another person," a possibility I had not considered before reading her book. She describes the process as a journey of self-discovery, opening doors to new cultures, perspectives, and ways of being.

Writer and essayist Pico Iyer, whom I cited in chapter three, beautifully captures in his essay "The Man Who Speaks Ten Languages" the emotional and personal rewards of language learning. He describes the way language unlocks connection and empathy, allowing us to "step into the minds and hearts of others."

And finally, novelist and translator Barbara Kingsolver, in her novel *The Lacuna*, explores the power of language to bridge cultural divides and foster understanding. Her protagonist learns Portuguese, and in so doing discovers new worlds and forges meaningful connections with people from different backgrounds.

My own experience of learning German was often much more prosaic than the happy outcomes promised by these writers. I was somewhat surprised, in fact, when I eventually passed my proficiency test. Reading German was for me always the easiest way to enjoy the language and still is. Beyond that, I could eventually understand what others were saying to me in conversation (and at the grocery store), and so hearing and understanding the language were usually not problems for me. On the other hand, forming sentences, learning to express myself, and saying what was on my mind continued to be challenges.

One time, because I wasn't feeling well, I made an appointment to see my *Hausartzt* (primary care physician), and I remember forming German sentences in my mind as I walked the few blocks to his office. Once inside the examining room, however, I stumbled and hesitated until the doctor said, in English, "Why don't you just tell me how you're feeling in your own words?" It was an unexpectedly humbling moment. I thought I was ready to communicate in the language of my host country and found that—at a crucial moment—I could not.

An unexpectedly happy experience of language learning occurred one Sunday morning at my church. It was Pentecost, and I had arranged with a few members of my church to call out "Come, Holy Spirit," at the beginning of worship—not spontaneously, and not all the same time, but one at a time and at my direction. The idea was that, with each voice, a different language would be heard and that we would be reminded of the miracle described in Acts 2 (when suddenly, after the sound of wind and the sight of fire atop the apostles' heads, everyone seemed to understand what the other was saying).

I found about twelve to fifteen volunteers who agreed to participate, and so at the beginning of worship I stood at the front and gestured toward the first person, who called out "Come, Holy Spirit" in French. And then, on and on it went—remarkably and beautifully, I thought—until it was over. Or, I should say, when it was supposed to be over.

Instead of ending where I had planned for this creative opening of worship to end, however, I heard more voices speaking in still other languages. Our church proudly claimed that more than two dozen nationalities and language groups were present on any given Sunday morning. The voice that drew unexpected laughter turned out to be the last one. An older man, a native Swiss and a person well known to all in the congregation, rose from his usual seat in the second row, turned to face the congregation, and spoke "Come, Holy Spirit" in Swiss German. That turned out to be a more appropriate and much more spontaneous end to that part of worship than the one I had planned. Of all the languages I thought to include that morning, I had somehow forgotten to include the unofficial language of our host country. I still think of the moment as a remarkable one, even a holy one. And as with all holy moments, it produced in me both wonder and tears.

In the first chapter, I noted that the Bible has a great deal to say about setting out. From Abraham in the Old Testament to Jesus in the New Testament, and of course to the Apostle Paul, whose various missionary journeys provide the outline for the Book of Acts, setting out is what people of faith often do, usually in response to God's call or the Spirit's prompting. And from the beginning, the challenges and possibilities of language have been a part of our human story. From the Tower of Babel in Genesis, where language ultimately divides the world—to a new kind of harmony of languages at Pentecost in the New Testament Book of Acts, language is a potential barrier or a doorway through which the Spirit can blow like that wind in Acts.

Jesus himself once said that he came with a message "for those with the ears to hear."

What I have tried to illustrate is that hearing the voice of the other takes time, commitment, sensitivity, even vulnerability. And, when the other is a stranger, coming together almost surely means a call to learn the other's language.

II

Reframing the Art of Travel

> *"A danger of travel is that we see things at the wrong time, before we have had a chance to build up the necessary receptivity and when new information is therefore as useless and fugitive as necklace beads without a connecting chain."*
>
> **Alain de Botton, *The Art of Travel***

Dad was an artist. He was a watercolorist, a form of painting that originated in China in the second century BCE. To be more specific, he was a hyperrealistic watercolor painter, making use of a dry brush and (frequently) a razor blade to achieve a near-photographic quality to his paintings. He painted in a style known as "transparent watercolor," which means that he did not use white or opaque paint. The style he chose certainly matched his exacting and perfectionist nature. I inherited much of that perfectionism though, sadly, none of his artistic abilities.

Early in his painting career, he became a "signature member" of the American Watercolor Society and a few other similar societies, and he began adding "AWS" to his name whenever he signed one of his paintings. He was proud of this distinction—better, in his mind, than a PhD because fewer were awarded. I remember taking the train from Princeton, where I was living at the time, to New York City, to see an exhibit with the painting that finally qualified him for membership. My wife took a photo of me standing in front of my dad's painting.

Like many children, I started to become aware in adulthood about how I was raised and how different it was from the way other children were raised. I could do without the perfectionism, of course, but the rest I have come to appreciate as a gift. Dad's drawing board took up a considerable amount of space in a corner of the family room, but when he was home that's where he could be found. My sisters and I learned to respect this space. Some fathers had workbenches with tools; my father had a drawing board with brushes and paints.

Dad's art has shaped to a considerable degree the way I approach art today. I remember going as a child to lots of art exhibits. I assumed that all children did and was surprised in adulthood when I found out that few if any of my friends and their families did. Our family sometimes drove hundreds of miles to see an exhibit, if it promised to be exceptionally good, and we used to go with a sense of anticipation and excitement, as if we were driving across the state to see a Detroit Tigers baseball game (which we also did each summer).

So, viewing art for me always began with the idea that this experience could be special—even unique. Artists had something to say, and I learned that we should pay attention. But not uncritical attention. I don't remember that Dad was enthusiastic about very many of the paintings or sculptures or installations we saw. He could be quite critical, in fact, either standing in front of a piece or talking about it on the way home. I inherited some of that too.

Beyond that, we always learned something in advance about what we were going to see. We never stumbled into an exhibit without having done our homework. We knew the name of the artist, of course, and some of the artist's previous work. What I learned was that, when possible, one should always get ready to see art, much as I have come to approach Sunday worship. Intentionally, thoughtfully, prayerfully we prepare and, if we do, we are more likely to experience a revelation.

On summer vacations—those three-week road trips around the U.S. and Canada—Dad would take a camera. When I was old enough to take my own camera on those road trips, I found myself seeing as Dad did, always looking for the best angle, sometimes climbing on top of some rocks to get a better view, other times crawling around on the ground to find the most interesting perspective. Photography to Dad was a form of art, and what I learned was that the purpose of photography was not to let friends on social media know where I had been, but to find beauty in the world, perhaps for later enjoyment. Dad's photos often became the inspiration months later for a painting.

When I was a senior in college, I took an art history class, partly because Professor Edgar Boevé had a reputation as a fine teacher as well as a fine artist. I count it as one of the most memorable classes of my four years as an undergraduate, perhaps because of my early interest in art. I still remember Boevé standing in front of a screen with a painting projected on it and pointing the class to every line, shape, form, and color in that painting. He showed us how our eyes would be drawn from one part of the painting to another through the genius of the artist's composition. After taking the class, I confess, I have spent a good part of my adult life searching out the paintings I studied in that class.

Boevé, like my other professors at Calvin University, was a product of the same Dutch Reformed tradition that I was. His father was a Dutch Reformed pastor, as a matter of fact. But to me and to many of my classmates, he seemed to be more worldly than the rest of the faculty, precisely because of his love for art. He certainly showed us a bigger and more interesting world than the one we were shown in other classes. Over a teaching career that spanned more than thirty years, Boevé established the art department at Calvin and, with his wife, Ervina, an ongoing interest in both the arts and theater among the students, a rare achievement for a small Christian liberal arts college.

An introductory course in art history might suggest worldwide art history, but as it turned out the class focused much more narrowly on the history of Western art. I fully acknowledge that my own experience of art, beginning with Dad and continuing with Boevé, was primarily an experience with this rather narrow slice of the world's available art.

Nearly all my museum and gallery visits over the years have been to see the work of Western painters and sculptors, but I have intentionally branched out. I am happy to report that today I own a print by the Japanese artist Sadao Watanabe. The print depicts a scene from Jesus' parable about the good Samaritan, which transcends cultural boundaries.

How indelibly did Dad's and Boevé's influences mark my own aesthetics? While we were living in Zürich, Switzerland, my wife and I decided to visit the famous Christmas markets in France. So, one December we made the two-hour drive to Colmar, in the Alsace region of France, near the French-German border. I knew before setting out that while we were there, I would have to see the famous Isenheim Altarpiece which, as I was taught in my art history class, is displayed in the Unterlinden Museum in Colmar. It is Matthias Grünewald's largest work and considered by many to be his masterpiece. Shopping the Christmas markets in Colmar was a treat but seeing the Isenheim Altarpiece in person—and not on a screen in an art history classroom—turned out to be both thrilling and moving.

What I remember from Boevé's class is Grünewald's portrayal of John the Baptist standing at the foot of the cross as Jesus is being crucified. John points an impossibly long and bony finger at Jesus, who of course is at the center of the painting. Grünewald, I should note, has painted one of the most brutally realistic and spiritually powerful depictions of the crucifixion. Jesus' body is plainly covered with sores and wounds, his head surrounded by a particularly brutal crown of thorns, and his hands and feet are pierced, not with tiny nails, but with enormous spikes. Perhaps worst of all, Jesus' mouth is stretched in wordless agony.

John of course had been executed by Herod long before Jesus' crucifixion, but by placing John at the foot of the cross, the artist (Boevé explained to my class) was revealing a larger truth—namely, that John's entire life had been about pointing toward the coming Messiah. And to make sure the viewer understands this point, Grünewald even paints the words from John 3:30 in Latin just above John's arm: "He must increase, but I must decrease."

To illustrate, Professor Boevé told us the story about the well-known twentieth-century Swiss theologian Karl Barth who had a print of Grünewald's painting on his office wall. According to Boevé, Barth would talk with visitors about the painting, and then he would often say, "I want to be that finger."

What are we pointing toward?

Perhaps you can see that Dad and Boevé, to some extent, became that finger for me. They pointed me toward how to see and listen and move and use as many senses as possible while traveling around the world—particularly when encountering the concentrated energy represented in works of art.

As a result, one of the most important lessons I have learned is that these experiences are ephemeral. Yes, Michelangelo's David stands after many centuries pretty much unchanged—but Michelangelo's work at the Vatican has, indeed, changed. And, when I go to the Netherlands today, I cannot visit Grandma Minnie's Netherlands.

Have your own travels to the Middle East taken you to Istanbul and what is now known as the Hagia Sophia Grand Mosque? When I walked into that World Heritage site, it was a museum. Completed in 537 CE, it was an Eastern Orthodox church until

1204 CE, when it was converted to a Roman Catholic church following the fourth crusade. It was reclaimed in 1261 CE as an Eastern Orthodox church until the Ottoman conquest of what was then Constantinople in 1453. It then served as a mosque until 1935 when it was reopened as a museum of the secular Republic of Turkey. In 2020 this major cultural and historical site reverted to being a mosque. While I can go back to the site itself—and much of the priceless art laden with sacred meaning still surrounds all facets of this architectural masterpiece—I cannot today reexperience "the museum" I once visited. Maybe that's good. Current Türkiye leaders seem to think so; other critics around the world don't. I'm not taking sides on this transition—simply pointing out that one of the timeless truths about the ancient Hagia Sophia is that it never stays the same.

The Papal Basilica of Saint Peter in the Vatican—more familiarly known as Saint Peter's Basilica—is an extraordinary place to visit, as any traveler to Rome will report. Construction of the basilica began in 1506 CE, but it wasn't completed until 1626, more than a century later. I have been to the Vatican several times to see it—with tour groups as well as members of my family. Even though I am not Catholic, I nevertheless feel a sense of wonder and awe every time I am there. I happened to be at the Vatican on Ash Wednesday many years ago, and I was present for then-Pope John Paul II's Wednesday audience in the Paul VI Audience Hall, along with about six thousand other noisy pilgrims. The pope offered greetings in several languages, and each time a language group heard the greeting in their language, the group would erupt in cheers and applause. When I heard the pope's greeting in English, I cheered as excitedly as everyone else.

Have your travels taken you to Rome? While most of the great monuments, altars, and artwork may seem unchanged, visitors around the world talk about the vast transformation of the Sistine Chapel after restoration of the frescoes was completed in 1994.

We can't go back and experience the shadowy mysteries of the sooty old chapel—not that we should prefer that over the cleaned version of Michelangelo's masterpiece. But our pilgrimages today to that sacred site are different from those of visitors for a century before these frescoes were lightened considerably.

As a product of the Protestant Reformation, I am happy to report that I have visited the major churches in Europe associated with the Reformation—beginning with the Schlosskirche (or Castle Church) in Wittenberg, Germany, where Martin Luther posted his *Ninety-five Theses* and launched the Protestant Reformation. In Zürich, Switzerland, I served a church for nearly five years which was within easy walking distance of the Grossmünster, where the Swiss reformer Huldrych Zwingli was pastor. The twin towers of the Grossmünster are perhaps the most recognized landmark in the city. And then, in Geneva, Switzerland, I have visited the St. Pierre Cathedral, where another Swiss reformer—John Calvin—once preached. I would have climbed the steps to his pulpit, but a rope and a sternly worded sign kept me from going up.

According to several accounts, the enraged citizens of Geneva, at the time of the Reformation, stripped the St. Pierre Cathedral, which had been a Roman Catholic church, of its rood screen (the ornate partition which separates the people from the place where the Mass is celebrated), its side chapels, its statues, as well as all decorative works of art except for the stained glass, pulpit, and some paintings at the tops of pillars. What was left was a plain interior that contrasts markedly with other medieval churches in Europe. I mention all of this here because I was shaped and formed in the Calvinist branch of the Reformation—which, let's say, has had a complicated relationship to art.

Perhaps you have been drawn to this kind of Protestant pilgrimage? What you may not immediately understand, however, is that all of these places have changed, and are changing in subtle ways. Imagine if you had visited St. Pierre in March 2022 and found yourself experiencing a lovely Catholic Mass in the church. Such a liturgy had not been celebrated there in nearly five hundred years, but an elaborate Mass took place that spring as a sign of ecumenical hospitality.

So, what exactly are we pointing toward when we tell others about our travels and hope they might someday have similar experiences? Are we even aware of the changes—small and large—taking place all the time? How do we feel about those changes? Remember that Grünewald himself felt that he could take the liberty of reenvisioning the holy crucifixion scene—inserting a figure who could not possibly have been there.

In powerful ways, our experience of travel to historic and artistic landmarks is ephemeral, partly because the sites themselves change over time—and partly because our own experiences, intentions, and emotions change as we encounter them.

I realize in retrospect that Dad's own enthusiastic embrace of art instinctively included this truth that the realm of art is larger—we might say more spiritually mysterious—than any literal "reading" could hope to capture. Dad did understand that his approach to art was a sharp departure from the norms and expectations in which he was raised. Dad designed the stained-glass windows for the church of my childhood in Grand Rapids where he and my mom were early, though not charter, members, and he would sometimes help our pastor with banners for a sermon series, but most of his art was not overtly or explicitly Christian. And, for that, he sometimes was criticized in his Dutch Reformed circles for not being a "Christian artist"—in other words, not being intentional with Christian images and themes, which is ironic given this history. He was irritated by the criticism, of course, but would usually say, by way of explanation, that he was "a Christian who happened to be an artist."

As far as I know, Dad never read Jacques Maritain's famous essay, "Christian Art," but he often verbalized the ideas and sentiments found there. He would have especially loved Maritain's line, "If you want to make a Christian work, then be a Christian, and simply try to make a beautiful work, into which your heart will pass; do not try to 'make Christian [art].'"

In suggesting that you, my reader companions, "look deeper" at what we're all "pointing toward" in this chapter, I certainly am not claiming to be a gifted visionary or master interpreter of the arts. While I am happy to report that I have been to nearly all of the major museums in Europe and have seen all the paintings that Professor Boevé introduced me to, I wonder about many of these museum visits. As Agnes Callard points out in "The Case Against Travel," most museum visitors spend little time in front of the paintings they have come to see. Even in the case of the "Mona Lisa," which can be viewed at the Louvre in Paris, most visitors apparently spend no more than fifteen seconds in front of the painting. Much of the reason for that, of course, is that the crowds most days prevent lingering.

When I went to live and work in The Hague, I remember racing over—*on my very first weekend!*—to the Mauritshuis Museum where the "Girl with the Pearl Earring" by Johannes Vermeer is part of the permanent collection. Though the number of people was much smaller that day than most, I remember feeling some pressure to keep walking, to avoid lingering in front of the painting, and to stand aside so that others could see it. The painting was moving—don't get me wrong—and I am so pleased to have seen it at last, but the experience was revealing. I learned early in my life to pay attention to art, to do my best to understand what the artist was saying to me, but for much of my life I have had the same experience that I had that day at the Mauritshuis.

What I long for, but what has happened too seldom in my life, is what happened to the Dutch Catholic priest and theologian Henri Nouwen. As he tells the story, he was visiting a friend in France in 1983 when he saw a wall print of Rembrandt's "The Return of the Prodigal," an unexpectedly large painting that depicts a scene from Jesus' parable of the prodigal son. Seeing the wall print deeply affected Nouwen. He reports that it made him want to "laugh and cry at the same time." He had just concluded a six-week lecture tour and was exhausted, and something about the painting revealed to Nouwen what he most needed.

Two years after seeing that Rembrandt print, Nouwen resigned his teaching position at Harvard University and returned to France. Nouwen was about to make a major life transition—from a Harvard teaching appointment to something still unclear to him—and he found himself continuing to think about the wall print. In his words, "the yearning for a lasting home ... grew deeper and stronger, somehow [turning] the painter [Rembrandt] into a faithful companion and guide."

Nouwen had the opportunity to travel to Saint Petersburg not long after, and not surprisingly, he visited the State Hermitage Museum where the Rembrandt original now hangs. Over a period of four days Nouwen spent hours in front of the painting. A close friend and museum guide found him a comfortable chair, and he sat looking at the painting, making notes about it, and listening to the comments of guides and visitors who passed in front of the painting. And then of course he wrote the influential bestseller *The Return of the Prodigal Son: A Story of Homecoming*, which is partly a reflection on the parable of Jesus, but also very much a reflection on Rembrandt's interpretation of it.

Yet that was not the end of the evolution of that artwork. Nouwen transformed Rembrandt's imagery into a new kind of guided spiritual experience for readers. Nouwen went on to deliver talks and lead retreats based on his inserting himself into the Bible-story-transformed-into-an-artwork. Then, Nouwen approved letting some of his followers travel with the book and usually with a big print of Rembrandt's painting that would be set up in front of audiences—congregations or circles of men and women on retreat. These trained facilitators inserted themselves into a Bible-story-turned-artwork-turned-spiritual-epiphany-for-the-prophetic-Nouwen-turned-mentor to future facilitators.

This constantly evolving experience all sprang from Nouwen's decision to spend so much time sitting near Rembrandt's painting.

Few people could accomplish what Nouwen achieved—but—well, do you see where I'm pointing now? Think about this for a moment, before we hurry back to our seats on the buses idling outside—or, in this case, before you turn these pages to the next chapter. I want to leave you with two more anecdotes to ponder—one funny, the other sobering.

One year, I received a study grant from the Louisville Institute/Lily Endowment, and the church I was serving at the time granted me a three-month summer sabbatical, which I used to take my wife and two teenage daughters to Italy. We saw all the museums and cathedrals that most tourists see in Milan, Florence, Venice, and Rome, but we also visited the ancient cities of Pompeii and Herculaneum—or at least what is left of them after the eruption of nearby Mount Vesuvius in 79 CE. The excavation at Pompeii and Herculaneum was so interesting that we followed up with a visit to the National Archaeological Museum in Naples, which was a short drive away.

At the time we were there, the museum was offering—in addition to its permanent collection—a special exhibit of "erotic art" recovered in the excavation. Our Italian language skills were minimal, so we missed the signs at the entrance and were puzzled when we were asked to sign a release allowing our underage daughters to enter the special exhibit. Once inside, to our embarrassment, we discovered the focus of this special exhibit.

Because the volcanic eruption left Pompeii and Herculaneum in such a well-preserved state, excavators have been able to recover an extensive collection of artifacts—such as statutes, frescoes, and household items, many of them decorated with sexual themes.

Clearly, the treatment of sexuality was far more relaxed in ancient Rome than it is in current Western culture. Brothels, baths, and private homes were filled with explicit sexual imagery. I am sure my daughters learned a great deal from the visit. I know I did.

And then this final story: When I raced over to the Mauritshuis Museum in The Hague to see "The Girl with the Pearl Earring," what I did not expect to see was new signage near the entrance of the museum acknowledging the role Count Johan Maurits played in the transatlantic slave trade.

Maurits, whose private residence in The Hague is now a well-known museum bearing his name, used his income from a plantation in Brazil to build his home and to assemble an extraordinary collection of art, including many Rembrandts. At least 24,000 enslaved Africans were transported to Brazil during his time as governor in order to keep his sugar mills running. In addition to signs that acknowledge the role of the slave trade in making the museum possible, the Mauritshuis has also gathered several paintings and one sculpture that had been scattered throughout the museum and assembled them on the first floor, so that visitors to the museum can form a new impression of Maurits, who had previously been regarded as an enlightened and benevolent governor.

In one of those paintings, now positioned close to the entrance, a young white woman is portrayed as a kind of princess, while a Black boy in the foreground is reduced to an exotic accessory. His presence in the painting underscores the exaltedness of the white woman. This painting and those nearby reveal important truths, though not the ones originally intended by the painters.

Throughout Europe, at the end of the twentieth and the beginning of the twenty-first century, a historic reckoning continues to sweep through historical sites and museums. Cultural artifacts are being returned to the countries where they were acquired or plundered through colonial rule. Many museums, like the

Mauritshuis, have legacies rooted in colonialism. Their collections were often received from wealthy donors who benefited from colonial empires. It is important that that truth be told as well.

Now, we're ready to move on to our next stop!

Watch your step! There are stumbling stones ahead of you—right there, right in the middle of the street—if you are visiting the right town and looking in the right directions.

12

Stolpersteine: Stumbling Stones

"The question shouldn't be 'Why are you, a Christian, here in a death camp, condemned for trying to save Jews?' The real question is 'Why aren't all the Christians here?'"

Joel C. Rosenberg, *The Auschwitz Escape*

Are we opening our eyes?

Stolpersteine certainly opened my eyes to the meaning and potential for public art that becomes deeply interwoven in our life's journeys.

I spent much of July 2016 at the Goethe Institute in Berlin, learning to speak German, a requirement for my Swiss work permit. But during lunch breaks I walked the streets near the institute and discovered that the cobblestone sidewalks were filled with 10-by-10 centimeter brass plates. Like Moses, who once felt compelled "to turn aside and see," I too found myself startled. I knelt, as if in prayer, and noticed that the plates had names and dates—and much more.

I soon realized that these brass plates can be found all over Berlin, and my curiosity led me to read as much as I could about these *Stolpersteine*, as they are known (literally, "stumbling stones"). The plates are not raised, which means they're not literally a tripping hazard. They are mounted nearly flush with the sidewalks where I found them, but their name suggests that people might stumble over them, which is what happened to me. The name *Stolpersteine* is also a reference to an old antisemitic remark. In Nazi Germany, if someone accidentally stumbled over a protruding stone, that person might say, "A Jew must be buried here." In other words, this idea has roots in a slur.

From the German I was learning at the institute, I was able to translate what I was reading on the plates: "Here lived Irma Rosenthal, born in Loewenberg 1910, deported 1943, murdered in Auschwitz." The two plates next to Irma's plates were for her daughters—Karla and Ellen, also deported to and then murdered in Auschwitz. The plates were placed in the sidewalk outside their last known address. They were taken from their home, and they never returned. Irma, the mother, died at age thirty-three, Karla at age fourteen, and Ellen at age ten.

In 2005, sixty years after the end of World War II, Germany opened a "Memorial to the Murdered Jews of Europe." Though visually striking, it was in some ways much like other war memorials—easy to ignore. You could spend time there if you wanted, but you could avoid it too. No one can avoid the *Stolpersteine*, especially not in a city like Berlin, which had one of the largest Jewish populations in Europe before World War II. *Stolpersteine* are a form of public art that commands our attention.

The first *Stolperstein* was created and installed by the German artist Gunter Demnig in 1992. Demnig's father, it seems important to note, was a soldier in the German army. Unlike other war memorials, *Stolpersteine* are designed to startle passersby and make them think about both the victims and the crimes committed against them, which once again is what happened to me.

Demnig has said that he wanted to create a memorial that would be "invisible but present," that would "touch people's hearts." Most war memorials can be found in a central location. Berlin's "Memorial to the Murdered Jews of Europe," for example, is immediately adjacent to the Brandenburg Gate, as well as the Tier

Garten, Berlin's largest and best-known park. *Stolpersteine*, on the other hand, are decentralized, spread throughout much of Berlin as well as Europe. *Stolpersteine* have been described in a 2008 documentary as the largest decentralized monument and art project in the world.

By 1992, fifty years had passed since the start of the Holocaust. To commemorate this anniversary, Demnig installed the first *Stolperstein* in front of Cologne's City Hall. The number of installations continued to grow, and in May 2023 the 100,000th *Stolperstein* was installed—in Nuremberg, in memory of Johann Wild, a Jewish firefighter. *Stolpersteine* today can be found in 1,200 cities in twenty-six countries throughout Europe. All plates are placed at the last known address of someone who was arrested, deported, and murdered by the Nazis—Sinti and Roma, Jews, Jehovah's Witnesses, homosexuals, mentally and/or physically disabled people, political dissenters, prostitutes, and others. The installations continue, and Demnig has been present for nearly all of them.

I moved back to the U.S. in 2018, but I did not forget the *Stolpersteine*. I continued to think about them and why they had made such an impression on me. A few months before moving back to the U.S., my wife and I made a three-hour drive from our home near Zürich, Switzerland, to Dachau, now essentially a suburb of Munich, Germany. Dachau was the site of the first German concentration camp, and though it was not designed to be an extermination camp, approximately 32,000 documented deaths took place there. Also, ten thousand of the thirty thousand survivors were seriously ill or near death when the camp was liberated.

After all the museums and cathedrals my wife and I had visited in Europe, this was our first visit to something related to World War II. Not surprisingly, this visit produced the most long-lasting memories of any sightseeing we did. The visit to Dachau was an important reason I continued to think about *Stolpersteine* after my return to the U.S.

Often war memorials are constructed to celebrate a great victory or to honor a heroic general, who might be depicted on horseback and resplendent in uniform. World War II has its share of such memorials, but perhaps because of the sheer number of civilian murders committed during this war, *Stolpersteine* are arguably a more fitting kind of memorial. Rather than the valorization of war and war heroes, *Stolpersteine* invite a deep engagement with the victims of war, those whose names might have been lost.

James E. Young, a Holocaust scholar, has described the way war memorials have changed over the course of the twentieth century. He calls the change a "counter-monument"—from "the heroic, self-aggrandizing figurative icons of the late nineteenth century … to the anti-heroic, often ironic and self-effacing conceptual installations marking the national ambivalence and uncertainty of late twentieth century post-modernism."

Certainly, in design and intent, Berlin's "Memorial to the Murdered Jews of Europe," fits this counter-monument description. The Vietnam Veterans Memorial in Washington, D.C., designed by the artist Maya Lin, is yet another example of this transformation. Not everyone was moved by the Vietnam memorial when it was first opened, and in subsequent years two far more traditional war monuments were installed nearby, evidence that the movement to counter-monument is not happening without some resistance.

It is important to note that the Vietnam memorial shares a few characteristics with Demnig's *Stolpersteine*. The use of names, for example. The Vietnam memorial has 58,320 names etched into black granite. To view the names, a visitor descends into what has been described as a "gash in the earth." To others the installation is symbolic of a "wound that is closed and healing." Unlike *Stolpersteine*, no other information—such as military rank or date of death—is provided on the monument along with the names.

I returned to Europe for the 2022–2023 school year, and in my first week back was startled once again to find *Stolpersteine*—this time in the neighborhood where I lived—in The Hague, Netherlands. I found two plates on the sidewalk where I walked to and from work each day, and once again, as I had in Berlin, I knelt to look more closely. As I did, I became aware that the *Stolpersteine* invite this sort of prayerful engagement. I brushed away some leaves and pine needles, I bent down to read carefully, and I experienced the same mixture of emotions that I did the first time I saw *Stolpersteine*.

The two brass plates I found were placed in front of a lovely, older row house, with the words (in Dutch):

> Here lived Robert K. Herrmann, born 1896, deported 1944, murdered January 16, 1945, Bergen-Belsen.
>
> Here lived Gertrude F.J.M. Herrmann-Katz, born 1901, deported 1944, murdered February 3, 1945, Bergen-Belsen.

Each time I passed that home, over the next nine months, I thought about Robert and Gertrude, who had once lived in my neighborhood, two people who might have waved to me as I walked to work. I imagined their lives on De Mildestraat, the name of their street. I gave thanks for them, and I lamented a world where the murder of millions of human beings might be planned and carried out with such brutality. To engage with *Stolpersteine*, I realized, can be an act of worship. But not worship as praise, joy, and thanksgiving. This form of worship requires confession, repentance, and remembering God's promise to redeem a broken world.

And there is more. In addition to inviting an act of worship, I found that *Stolpersteine* exist as a kind of accusation. Did any of the neighbors come to Robert and Gertrude's defense? Or, as often happened, did the neighbors look the other way? Looking back, many people might imagine themselves involved in the heroic work of resistance, but the truth is that in World War II there were many more collaborators than resisters. And so, *Stolpersteine* raise the question: What would I have done in similar circumstances? The names I saw serve as judgment to me and everyone else who refuses to speak on behalf of those who are unjustly treated, assaulted, and sometimes murdered.

Stolpersteine have generally been praised by art critics for their originality. They have done more than most memorials to raise awareness of the Holocaust. For some, though, the plates seem too small and insignificant. Some cities—Munich is the best known—have even passed ordinances banning the installation of *Stolpersteine*. The Munich decision was made after considerable debate, but in the end the *Stolpersteine* were determined to be "disrespectful" to Holocaust victims. As some have put it, a memorial that could be stepped on, stolen, or desecrated was not a fitting remembrance for the victims of the Holocaust.

Munich, because of its proximity to the first Nazi concentration camp, was prodded to devise other ways to honor victims of the Holocaust, and the city has done so. Victims' relatives must file a request with the city council for more suitable memorials. Plaques mounted on walls seem to be the most popular alternative. Rather than being offended when communities decide not to allow installations, Demnig seems pleased that a discussion has occurred. His art, in other words, has power and influence even in its absence.

Demnig claims no religious faith, but he has cited a line from the Talmud as an inspiration for his art: "A person is only forgotten when his or her name is forgotten." And so, one stone, one name, one person who will not be forgotten. Whether intended or not, Demnig has called attention to something important in the Christian tradition, where names are more than just labels or identifiers. For Christian people, names are often imbued with considerable significance. They are, among other things, closely linked to a person's identity.

When Jews and others were taken to concentration camps, they were not only stripped of their clothes, but their names were taken from them as well. If they were not murdered immediately after arrival, numbers were usually tattooed on their forearms. And so, *Stolpersteine* symbolically restore the names of the victims. In Isaiah 43:1, the prophet quotes God as saying, "Fear not, for I have redeemed you; I have called you by name." For God to remember each of us by name is intended to be a great comfort and a sign of the vastness of God's love. *Stolpersteine* point us toward this and other ways the Judeo-Christian tradition thinks about names.

Still another part of Demnig's artistic imagination was the decision not to mass produce the brass plates, but to make each one by hand—a clear contrast to what has been described as the "industrialized murder" of human beings by the Nazis. Omer Bartov, a Rutgers University scholar, uses the term to mean "the mechanized, impersonal, and sustained mass destruction of human beings, organized and administered by states, legitimized and set into motion by scientists and jurists, sanctioned and popularized by academics and intellectuals." To this way of thinking, Demnig has spoken a kind of rebuke in the way his art is created, produced, and crafted.

In an interview with a *New York Times* reporter, Demnig remarked that "it goes beyond our comprehension to understand the killing of six million Jews. But if you read the name of one person, calculate his age, look at his old home, and wonder behind which window he used to live, then the horror has a face to it." What I sense in this comment is Demnig's concern to help the ordinary person—attending language school in Berlin, for example—to connect to something so vast and so evil that it mostly defies description, let alone understanding. *Stolpersteine* help the person who stumbles on them to see and understand—perhaps briefly—how vast and how evil the Holocaust was.

Demnig is not the first artist in history to face this challenge to the artistic imagination. "Guernica," a mural-sized painting completed by Pablo Picasso in 1937 and now hanging at a museum in Madrid, attempts to depict the bombing of the Basque town of Guernica by German and Italian forces during the Spanish Civil War. To stand in front of it, to see the distorted figures and fragmented forms, is to experience at an emotional level some of the chaos and destruction of war. Picasso, however, never attempted the sort of public art that makes Demnig's *Stolpersteine* so powerful and unavoidable.

Christians in Germany have had a variety of responses to Demnig's work. The United Evangelical Lutheran Church of Germany, founded in 1948 after the end of World War II, has issued a statement that *Stolpersteine* are "a powerful reminder of the Holocaust" and that they "call us to remember the victims and to fight against all forms of hatred and resistance." Those words seem to me lacking in enthusiasm, but they do express a Christian truth about the importance of memory and the call to fight hatred.

The Roman Catholic Church in Germany has said that *Stolpersteine* are "a sacred act of remembrance" and that they "help us to keep the memory of the Holocaust alive and to work for a more just and peaceful world." The words "sacred act of remembrance" seem to me a recognition of the Christian imagination. When a Christian views public art—and this public art in particular—the Christian brings along an insight or point of view that allows for a recognition of the holy. This has been my experience with *Stolpersteine*. Whether or not Demnig is a Christian seems not to matter. I have seen something in his work that awakens in me a sense of the sacred. Not the plate itself—or even the words inscribed on it—but what the plate asks me to envision and confess. These were human beings created in the image and likeness of God, they were murdered, and I did not speak up for them.

The Protestant Church in Germany, formerly known as the Evangelical Church in Germany, has said that *Stolpersteine* are a "call to action" and that they "challenge us to stand up against all forms of discrimination and persecution." I find it significant that all three of these major religious bodies in Germany have felt compelled to issue statements about an art installation. I can think of no other art that has compelled a country's leading Christian churches to respond, to issue a statement, to say something in response.

What adds urgency to the *Stolpersteine* project in Europe is that both Germany and Poland have faced in recent years the rise of far-right political groups that have sought to diminish or gloss over the importance of the Nazi era. The argument is that too much attention on World War II stands in the way of a renewed national pride. A leader of the Alternative für Deutschland (AfD) political party once described the Nazi era as a "speck of bird poop" in Germany's otherwise admirable history. Another far-right leader has called Berlin's Memorial to the Murdered Jews of Europe a "monument of shame" and says Germany should stop apologizing for Nazi crimes. For now, though, Germany remains serious about reckoning with its history. High school students are required to take classes on twentieth-century German history, including the Nazi era and the Holocaust, but for now visiting a concentration camp is not compulsory for German students.

Demnig's project causes me to ponder U.S. history, especially with the rise of our own far-right political groups. Public art like *Stolpersteine* can challenge the historical narrative—or what we prefer the national narrative to be.

In 2018, the National Memorial for Peace and Justice (known informally as the "National Lynching Memorial") opened in Montgomery, Alabama, on a six-acre site overlooking the Alabama State Capitol. The memorial is dedicated to the victims of American white supremacy, and—like *Stolpersteine*—the memorial demands a reckoning with one of the worst atrocities in U.S. history: the lynching of thousands of Black people. From 1882 to 1968, the NAACP has determined that 4,743 lynchings occurred in the U.S. in a campaign of racist terror. Mississippi had the largest number of lynchings with 581. Georgia was next with 531. And Texas was third with 493. Only seven states had no recorded lynchings during the period—Arizona, Idaho, Maine, Nevada, South Dakota, Vermont, and Wisconsin.

At the memorial there are eight hundred weathered columns, all hanging from the roof. Etched on each column is the name of an American county and the names of the people who were lynched there. Some are noted simply as "unknown." The memorial is constructed so that, as one walks along, the floor slowly descends. By the end, the columns are dangling, leaving the viewer in the position of one of the white spectators shown in old photographs of public lynchings.

Some public art makes us uncomfortable but compels us to look and engage with it. The memorial in Montgomery has made me profoundly uncomfortable, but more than that, I find that it calls forth a response. The call I hear is that something like this must never be allowed to happen again, that I must find within myself the courage to speak and act on behalf of those who have been unjustly judged and condemned. And yet, I worry that the response of Christian people like me will be something like the response of the United Evangelical Lutheran Church to *Stolpersteine*—simply calling it "a powerful reminder" and not much more.

13

There's No Place Like 'Home'

"You know you are truly alive when you're living among lions."
Isak Dinesen (Karen Blixen), Out of Africa

At this point, you know me and my family fairly well, but my guess is that you can't predict where this chapter is going.

I couldn't, and I was the traveler.

Let me see. Where to begin?

Well, I was startled myself when I learned that Dad, at age fifty-nine, decided to sell his advertising business and paint full time. He had returned from World War II at age twenty or twenty-one and, wanting to take advantage of the GI Bill, was accepted at the School of the Art Institute of Chicago, but his admission was delayed one semester—from September to January—because of the large number of returning veterans. During those months he met and started dating the woman who would become my mom. So, he decided against moving to Chicago, in favor of marriage and an entry level position at the Jaqua Advertising Agency in Grand Rapids, Michigan.

He worked at Jaqua for nearly forty years, moving from artist to creative director and finally to president, winning awards along the way, working long hours, and at the end owning a majority share of the company. Something happened along the way, though, and at age fifty-nine he was ready to be finished with all of it. I never asked him in detail about what led to his decision, but it seems clear that he wanted at long last to do something that he had always loved, something that was his own worthy adventure. And that was to become an artist.

Dad's gift for drawing was evident at an early age. I have seen one of his early drawings, and the level of his skill is astounding. His mother could see his gift too, but she felt compelled to tell him that "you can't make a living as an artist." He listened to this advice and put off his dream. Dad's work at Jaqua, I realize, made possible all those summer road trips that made such an impression on me, just as it made possible the travel he did throughout his life, but there must have been something deeply unsatisfying about it too.

That's my guess because I now see that something similar happened to me.

For my fiftieth birthday, I ran what I am almost certain will be the last marathon of my life. I somehow found a Saturday morning race—a rare thing in the world of marathoning—a race that was within driving distance of the Chicago suburbs where I lived. A Saturday race was important because I had to be at work the next morning, preaching a sermon and leading worship at my church. It never occurred to me that I might be too sore on Sunday morning to climb a few steps to reach the church's old pulpit. I made it but not without wincing on the way up.

And then, on Sunday afternoon, my wife and I flew from Chicago's O'Hare Airport to Milan's Malpensa Airport for a week worthy of our five decades of life (Susan's birthday was just a couple of months after mine). After landing, we took a forty-five-minute taxi ride to a hotel on Lake Como. The weather at the end of October was beautiful, but for some reason there weren't many people around. Our plan had been to take a cooking class, but before the first class we decided that what we really wanted to do was to eat someone else's cooking and enjoy ourselves.

So, that's what we did. Most days we took a water taxi around the lake, stopped at a variety of hotels, shopped, and sampled northern Italian cuisine. On an expectedly warm day, we took the water taxi to a nearby monastery, where we spent the afternoon outdoors, having a picnic lunch, reading, and napping on the lovely grounds.

A visit to the Lake District of Italy had not been on any list of places I wanted to see. The decision to go was entirely spontaneous, which can make travel fun. During one particularly long Chicago winter, my wife and I looked for inexpensive airfares to Mexico, hoping for a short warm weather getaway, only to find a few even less expensive airfares to the southern coast of Spain—the Costa del Sol—where we ended up instead.

By that point in my life, I had acquired lots of stamps in my passport. I had learned to overlook the inevitable headaches of travel and to focus instead on the lovely surprises—like being able to pop over to Africa for a day of shopping in the outdoor markets. This sense of adventure, however, had not found its way to other parts of my life. I was still doing what I learned from my parents—taking road trips now and then to satisfy what I have described as my adventure gene. But the rest of my life was far from the adventure that I craved. At mid-career I was unhappy. I was happy about being a pastor, and couldn't imagine another career, but parts of my work were deeply unsatisfying. I loved the deep connections that life in a church makes possible, but I was struggling. So, I made an appointment with someone who made a living as a counselor to unhappy pastors. He put me through a battery of vocational tests, he asked me to write an essay on what I considered to be my major accomplishments, and then we sat down to talk about all of it. Toward the end of our time together, I remember him saying, "It sounds as though you want to get back to whatever it was you originally felt called to do." In other words, whatever it was that made me think I was suited to the life of a pastor in the first place.

On the drive home, I remember thinking that I had made a significant breakthrough. But I quickly realized that I had more work to do. How did I ever let myself drift so far from the joy I felt earlier in my work? The issue, I slowly began to realize, was that I had allowed my ambition to become an all-consuming feature of my life. Not worthy adventure, but bigger and bigger churches. I found myself with large staffs and budgets that did not raise themselves. I would spend my time supervising the people employed by the church and then raising the money to pay their salaries. I was not exactly miserable, but I was far from those things that had excited me at the beginning. Attending meetings to review bids for roof repair did not spark joy in me.

Another ten years would pass before I did something about it. After that session with the counselor, I served two more churches, which may have looked impressive on my resume, but which were not good for me. I was nearing my sixtieth birthday and living in Fort Lauderdale, Florida, when someone asked me if I had ever thought about living and working in Europe. I had no idea at the time that there were English-speaking churches in Europe (and throughout the world). But there were, and I soon learned that they preferred native English speakers to be their pastors. A church in Zürich, Switzerland, I was told, was looking for a new pastor.

Would I be interested in applying?

I heard myself say, "Yes, I would," and so I applied.

I very soon became one of two finalists for the position. My wife and I flew to Switzerland over a Fourth of July holiday, and no one except for a neighbor who took care of our dog knew that we had been away. I preached a sermon for the congregation in Zürich, I engaged in a memorable question-and-answer session with the congregation, and a week later they took a vote and invited me to be their next pastor, a fifty-nine-year-old American and his wife who had never lived outside the U.S.

The next several months were a blur of activity. I had no idea how much is involved in moving to another country. We said goodbye to our Fort Lauderdale church and to those lovely sub-tropical winters, we sold our house, we put most (but not all) of our furniture and household goods in storage, we sold one car and put the other (a nearly new one) in storage, and we traveled to the Swiss consulate in Chicago to apply for visas. Then we waited. Somewhere during the waiting period, I led yet another pilgrimage to Israel, a tour I had committed to before deciding to move to Switzerland. I did not arrive for work in Switzerland until the following January.

What everyone told me—but what I could not have anticipated—was how different it is to live in another country, as opposed to, say, living out of a suitcase and driving around in a rental car. My wife and I found an apartment in a small village outside Zürich, a fifteen-minute train ride to a station very close to the church, but had to wait until we were approved. In Switzerland, finding an apartment is complicated, as is just about everything else—especially for people who are arriving from another country. Once we were approved, though, a shipping container with our household goods quickly made its way across the Atlantic, arrived at the port in Antwerp, Belgium, and was delivered to our apartment.

We met our neighbors, most of whom were very friendly, but they were also alert to any infractions of both written and unwritten rules of conduct, often having to do with making noise on Sunday. An early joke we learned was that Switzerland has nine million police (which is roughly the population of the country), and each one feels obliged to monitor the behavior of the other nine million. Our neighbors never hesitated to let us know when we had broken the rules, though they always did it with a smile, as if to say, "Just being helpful!"

One of the differences I noticed early on between this new culture and the one I left behind is that having a car wasn't strictly necessary. In fact, having a car is often more of a nuisance than a convenience. I discovered that I could get anywhere in the country by taking a train, bus, or tram, often a combination of the three. Nearly everyone uses public transportation. Even the president of the country while I was there (Switzerland rotates the position among members of a federal council), waited at the train station in the morning, along with everyone else.

But we were Americans, after all, and eventually we bought a car—a big one. European cars tend to be smaller than their American counterparts, so we found the biggest European model we could find—a twenty-year-old Volvo station wagon, the color of a deep thigh bruise—and we used it to travel all over western Europe.

I don't remember ever seeing the police make a traffic stop during my years in Switzerland. They apparently have more important things to do. Driving is monitored by cameras and radar. I discovered this arrangement within the first week of car ownership, when I drove down a city street where the speed limit was clearly marked as thirty kilometers per hour (a painfully slow eighteen miles per hour). A camera/radar device positioned next to the road noted my speed and took a photo of my license plate. Within a few days a letter arrived in the mail letting me know about my fine which, I must say, was substantial. After two fines in one week, I either avoided that street or drove very slowly. Lesson learned.

The Swiss are notoriously hard workers. In fact, they will be happy to explain this to you, in case you had not heard. A century ago, Max Weber tried to trace their work ethic to the Reformation roots in Switzerland. Human value, the Reformers seemed to say, was measured by hard work, thrift, and efficiency. So, during work hours the Swiss will typically do prodigious amounts of work. But after work hours? Don't expect anyone to respond to an email.

What we discovered was that the strong Swiss work ethic was balanced by an equally strong commitment to family time.

Evenings, weekends, and holidays? These were dedicated to pursuits such as hiking (the national pastime), skiing (the national sport), or spending time in the *Schrebergarten* (which translates to "hobby garden"). Nearly seventy percent of Swiss people live in apartments, not private homes, and so to garden means renting or buying a tiny garden plot in a community of such plots. Most of these plots also have a shed, and the Swiss often go to their tiny farms for an afternoon and evening of grilling, gardening, and wine-drinking—much like having a home at the lake.

Switzerland is beautiful, as anyone who has ever been to the country will tell you. The views are stunning in all directions. The northern, German-speaking region where we lived is particularly gorgeous. Our village was located on the north side of Lake Zürich about midway between Zürich and Rapperswil. Our side of the lake is known as the "gold coast" because of the warm afternoon sun, and our apartment building was surrounded by vineyards which must have produced a considerable amount of wine. All but two percent of the wine produced in the country, however, is consumed within the national borders. To hear the Swiss sheepishly concede that theirs is perhaps not the world's best wine is surprising in a country that aspires to be the best at everything from banking to watchmaking.

I have started men's groups in every church I have served, though never before an exercise group. A men's hiking group for the church in Zürich seemed like a natural choice. And so, one Saturday each month, twelve to twenty men gathered in the church basement and then set off, usually by train, to a nearby mountain or well-known trail. One Saturday we hiked to the top of Grosser Mythen, an iconic rocky outcrop which dominates the landscape on the eastern side of Lake Lucerne. From the base of the mountain to the peak requires a walk of over two kilometers, with a gain of over four hundred meters in elevation (over 1,300 feet) and forty-six hairpin turns. It is a challenging but gratifying climb, and most of the Swiss people I knew claimed to have made the climb at least once in their lives.

My favorite hiking memory is reaching the top of Grosser Mythen, wearing my University of Michigan baseball cap, and hearing someone (who turned out to be another Michigan native) say, "Go Blue!" At the top of most mountains there seemed to be restaurants, which were ideal for lunch and a stout German beer before we would start our descent. On those Saturdays when the men's hiking group did not meet, I often took my dog to the Pfannenstiel, a mountain ridge that borders Lake Zürich, and we would walk the trail for hours in all kinds of weather.

By far the biggest challenge of my five years in Switzerland was learning to speak the language: not *Schwiizerdürsch*, the Swiss German dialect spoken (proudly) by the locals—but *Hochdeutsch*, or standard German. The latter is one of the four official languages of Switzerland, and people like me who are allowed to live and work in the country are expected to learn one of the official languages. If I had lived in the western, French-speaking part of the country, I would have been required to learn French. In the south, bordering Italy, newcomers are required to learn Italian. In the far eastern part of the country, in a single canton known as Grisons, about sixty thousand people speak Romansh. The Swiss government spends about 7.6 million francs annually to promote and preserve Romansh, and it is taught in cantonal schools until the sixth grade, when German becomes the default language.

I am certain that if I had been six or seven years old when I moved to Switzerland, I would have become a fluent German speaker in a matter of months. Expats with young children sometimes enrolled them in German schools, and after a rough start most children quickly master the new language. Language learning for sixty-year-olds is more difficult, but I loved the challenge. Today the government requires that newcomers reach a relatively high level of proficiency in six months or so; when I started, the rules were much more relaxed. I attended weekly German language classes in my village, I listened to "slow German" *Deutsche Welle* news podcasts on the train, and I read one of the free daily newspapers—*Das Blick*—which I found at the train station. One summer, as I neared the date for my language proficiency test, I spent a few weeks at the Goethe Institute in Berlin. My instructors spoke German, my classmates spoke German, and mostly (because I had no choice) I spoke German, too.

One reason for making the trip to Berlin—there were lots of language schools closer to home—was that I had been asked to officiate at a wedding in Potsdam, a forty-five-minute train ride from Berlin. The church I served as pastor was an English-speaking church, and so I preached and led worship in English, but the young woman who asked me to officiate at her wedding was from a family that did not speak English. And so, she asked me to do half of the wedding in German and the other half in English. My instructor at the Goethe Institute helped me with my wedding preparation, in addition to my other work. I can report that no one at the wedding laughed or complained (or said much of anything) about my language abilities, but I can imagine that I was difficult to understand. The youth at my church in Zürich, who were much less polite, once covered their ears and asked me to speak English because, as one of them put it, "your German hurts our ears."

I enjoyed my years in Zürich. But that doesn't begin to describe the range of feelings that I had while living and working there. Every day, it seemed, I was stretched and challenged. Meeting people from so many other cultures made me a better listener and a closer observer than I had ever been, than I had ever imagined possible. Not that the experience was easy—much of the time it wasn't—but I felt engaged in every situation and every encounter. At any moment, it seemed, I would be expected to learn and adapt and reflect.

Zürich and the surrounding villages—what we in the U.S. might call "the greater Zürich area"—have a combined population of around 1.5 million, and a third of those people are not native born. (In smaller towns and rural areas, of course, there is much less diversity.) The non-Swiss population in greater Zürich comes from 172 different countries, which makes for an astonishing variety of stories and customs and adjustments. At the church I served, we typically counted more than two dozen nationalities and language groups on any given Sunday morning.

I had never worked in such a challenging environment. I can honestly say that my previous churches were easy to serve—at least by comparison. I knew my people in those other churches, and they knew me. We looked alike and talked alike, and we shared similar values. Our differences were miniscule compared to the cultural differences within the Zürich congregation. We all spoke English, true, though for many people in the church English was not a first language. We all shared a common faith too, but coming to faith in an Asian culture, say, is vastly different from coming to faith, as I did, in a Western culture.

All of this was wonderful—at least that's how I remember it. I even felt compelled to write a book about the multicultural experience. But what made my years in Zürich a kind of turning point in my life was something that happened one morning. I remember waking up with my teeth clenched, something that doesn't happen often, and I woke up thinking about a betrayal earlier in my life, a situation that hurt so much I was still carrying it with me, able to remember every dreadful part of it. And then, it occurred to me, as I was still lying in bed that morning, that the reason I was remembering what had happened was that I was finally ready to deal with it.

Something about finding congruence at last between my work and my life, something about the distance I had traveled and the experiences I had had along the way, allowed me to remember—and, this is important, to let it go, to forgive, to get on with my life. I was over sixty years old, waking up in an apartment near Zürich, Switzerland, and I knew in that moment that I had grown up, that I had finally arrived at a place of peace. I knew there were more adventures ahead of me, but I also knew that I had finally achieved what I most needed. Not one more museum, not one more famous cathedral, not even popping over to Africa for a day of shopping, but something inside of me.

That morning I felt as though I had finally become whole again. By letting go, of all things. By an act of forgiveness. By breathing deeply again.

If my life were mapped out on Joseph Campbell's "hero's journey" framework, then you might say that I had accomplished that one last, decisive act that would allow me to return home. I was comfortable with my life and career. I had not achieved perfection (my Calvinist faith formation prevents me from even entertaining the idea), but something was now different.

I could feel it as soon as I stopped clenching my teeth. The struggle was over.

I knew that my life in this place was worthy of the gifts I had been given.

14

The Romance of 'Barbarous Coasts'

"I love to sail forbidden seas, and land on barbarous coasts."
Herman Melville, Moby-Dick or, The Whale

Clarity. Forgiveness. Compassion. These were among the indelible values and experiences I was packing along with me for the long journey my wife and I would take back toward our roots in Michigan.

My wife and I had decided to enjoy our journey back to the States. One reason is that we were moving in January and did not want to face a frigid Michigan winter in a mostly deserted beach association where we had decided to build a retirement home. So, we decided to set out on a slow, pleasant journey that did not have to be a pilgrimage, or a mission trip, or even a study tour, though in many ways it was all of those things. We weren't keen on seeing more of Europe because we had seen so much of it already and, instead, we decided to revisit a country that had intrigued us more than fifteen years earlier: Morocco.

I remember thinking, "What an exotic blend of cultures in a warm North African climate!" So, we booked our travel plans.

But in doing so, I was reminded: As much as we might like to simply set sail and enjoy the journey—a lifetime of thoughtful reflection on travel made us hyper-aware of our descent into some of the most infamous scenes of colonialist bias. Even that phrase—colonialist bias—makes me sad. All we wanted was a pleasant journey back to the Midwest, but the friction of our consciences would not let us overlook the lingering injustices in our world.

I blame Edith Wharton. And, if you are a Wharton fan, don't write to tell me that she was a feminist pioneer and heroic defender of social justice. I agree that she was truly a world-class traveler, having crossed the Atlantic more than sixty times. During World War I, instead of fleeing Paris in the panic over invading German forces, she stayed in the French capital where she helped a large number of unemployed and nearly destitute women find practical work. She organized refuges for refugees. She publicized the horrors of war in a series of highly praised articles for *Scribner's* magazine. And, after her post-war visit to Morocco—or, perhaps because of her visit to Morocco, some literary scholars say—she wrote the 1921 Pulitzer Prize-winning novel, *Age of Innocence*, a literary skewering of the unfair biases and constraints imposed by high society.

But in Morocco, Wharton struggled to find her footing and her journalistic voice. I came to realize this because, as a thoughtful traveler myself, I made it a point to read her often-overlooked memoir, *In Morocco*. One sign that this was not her finest work is that, among her dozen-plus books that have full-scale Wikipedia pages, *In Morocco* has not yet found any fans who have volunteered to build a Wikipedia page extoling its virtues.

What's flawed about *In Morocco*? We can start with Wharton's description of herself as an enthusiastic "imperialist." She took this tour of Morocco as a guest of French colonial officials, who she then praised in the magazine articles that formed the eventual book. This ethical lapse in her work as a journalist is an issue to this day among scholars who study and write about her legacy. For example, an extensive 2018 article about her Morocco adventures was commissioned by the National Endowment for the Humanities. In the final article, journalist Meredith Hindley bends over backward to remind readers of her many glowing qualities, but Hindley ultimately describes *In Morocco* as a "pro-colonial tract."

Perhaps I should have seen this experience coming, but Morocco seemed like such a delightful choice at the time. We knew a little bit about it. While visiting the Costa del Sol in Spain earlier, we had taken the easy ferry ride to Tangier and had shopped in the markets there.

As we were charting a fresh destination for this journey, we wondered: What about the other cities in Morocco—Marrakech, Fez, Rabat, and Casablanca? What about the pristine beaches near Essaouira, which promised a beach holiday with warm sand and sunshine? What about the snow-capped Atlas Mountains and the vast Sahara Desert? Morocco not only has a diverse geography and great shopping but also, as we would learn, a complicated history.

When Americans think about Morocco, if they think about it at all, they summon scenes from the classic 1942 film, *Casablanca*, starring Humphrey Bogart (who played Rick Blaine, an American expat living in Morocco) and Ingrid Bergman (who played Ilsa Lund, a woman with whom Rick had a romantic involvement before she showed up unexpectedly in Casablanca). I loved that film for lots of reasons, but not so much for the love story. I loved it mostly because of its exotic location and the idea that an American could live in a place like Casablanca and run a business there and find adventure. Imagine how disappointed I was when I eventually learned that the entire film was shot at Warner Brothers Studios in Burbank, California. Even an airport scene, with Nazi villain Heinrich Strasser flying past an airport hangar, was shot at Van Nuys Airport in Los Angeles. Still, I dreamed of going to the real Casablanca one day—not to hang out at Rick's Café (which exists today "enchanting guests with its elegant atmosphere, intricate interiors, and captivating live piano music"), but to see the city for myself, a city known, among other things, for its extraordinary architecture.

What I didn't know then, and what the film did not reveal, is that Morocco, beginning with the ninth century BCE, was once part of several other empires. Archeological studies show that what is now Morocco was once part of a much wider Mediterranean trading world, brought together by the Phoenicians. Later, what is now Morocco became part of the northwestern African civilization of ancient Carthage, the Carthaginian Empire. That was eventually followed by the arrival of Berbers, Romans, and then Arab Muslims.

Today Islam is the official and predominant religion, a legacy of the Arab conquest, and Morocco defines itself as a Muslim state. But—like Turkey and parts of Bosnia—it retains an identity separate from other Arab countries. Morocco could be considered a moderate, perhaps even a secular country, in comparison to other Muslim-majority countries. Morocco seems proud, for example, of its rich history of co-existence between Muslims, Christians, and Jews. The government even promotes interfaith dialog, not a characteristic of most other Muslim-majority countries.

Our guide, a retired schoolteacher, took my wife and me on a walking tour around Marrakech and made a point of reassuring us about his secular perspectives. He showed up at the *riad* where we were staying (a traditional Moroccan home with an inner courtyard), wearing his djellaba, a loose-fitting hooded garment, resembling a kaftan, worn by both men and women. And since it was a cool day in January, the fabric of our guide's *djellaba* was noticeably heavier than I would have anticipated. It sure looked nice and warm! In both dress and attitude, our guide for the walking tour that day emphasized that he was not an Arab Muslim. He was something proudly different. Though he spoke Moroccan Arabic, a popular dialect in Morocco, he was also fluent in French, Berber, and English.

So what exactly is a Moroccan identity? As it turns out, that's hard to say.

By the late nineteenth and early twentieth centuries, both Spain and France had created what have been euphemistically called "zones of influence" in Morocco, Spain to the north and France to the south. More accurately, Spain and France were colonial powers who divided and ruled the country. It was not until 1956 that Morocco finally gained its independence from France and became the Kingdom of Morocco, changing from a sultanate to a kingdom. With so many empires, civilizations, and ruling powers, it is no wonder that Morocco seems "exotic" to Western tourists, including my wife and me. That word, as it turns out, gets used a great deal in connection with Morocco. The Moroccan people we talked to nearly always emphasized their Berber past, usually to distinguish themselves from their Arab conquerors, but the influence of other civilizations is obvious as well. It's a difficult country to describe, and even a few weeks of living there was not enough for me to offer a succinct description.

So, I have real sympathy for the challenge Wharton faced when she accepted the invitation of Hubert Lyautey, the governor general of what was then the French Protectorate of Morocco. He offered her VIP privileges wherever she traveled, including a car, driver, and what she described as "military assistance" for her safety when she traveled from city to city. Lyautey was undoubtedly hoping that Wharton would write favorably about the country—and especially about his rule—and she did not disappoint. She wrote glowingly of Lyautey as a wise and benevolent ruler, and she seemed to regard French rule overall as beneficial to Moroccans, saving them from themselves, as she put it. In all, Wharton had about a month in Morocco and then didn't have to finish her stories until the summer 1919 issue of *Scribner's*. So, she had a lot of time, back in France as the war ground onward, to draft and redraft her most dramatic accounts for the magazine. At one point in her adventures, she and the wife of Governor General Lyautey entered a harem, where they glimpsed "a princess out of an Arab fairy-tale." It's fair to say that Wharton sees the young women of the harem, not so much as human beings, but rather as objects to be examined, "exotic" creatures to be viewed.

At one point she describes the sultan's "favorites" within the harem: "[R]ound-faced apricot-tinted girls in their teens, with high cheekbones, full red lips, surprised brown eyes between curved-up Asiatic lids, and little brown hands fluttering out like birds from their brocaded sleeves." In other words, she sees these young women as "exotic"—that word again. To be fair, her attempts to speak with them were mostly unsuccessful. The single conversation she reports occurred only with the help of a male translator, and the young woman seemed wary of the encounter and fearful of the translator.

In other words, other cultures are often viewed by Westerners through a colonial gaze. Wharton, a product of her times as surely as I am a product of mine, saw Moroccan culture as inferior to French and American culture. What we can do today is to recognize that this problem of perception did not begin with Edith Wharton, and it will not end with this book. The classic manifesto identifying the way the colonial gaze denigrates especially Arab and Muslim cultures around the Mediterranean rim—the book *Orientalism* by the scholar Edward Said—was published in 1978. Before his death in 2003, Said still was publishing essays defending the relevance of his original warning.

I did count Wharton's book as helpful to my understanding of "our" Western relationship with Morocco—just as I have read Twain and come away with similar critiques about his bias. I have included them in my life and travels—and now in this book—because we need to encourage each other to guard against these limitations of perception.

A huge number of Americans are bound for Morocco right now. Since tourist spending brings in somewhere between five and nine billion U.S. dollars a year, an unfortunate kind of bargain seems to have been made: Morocco needs and depends on tourist dollars, and in exchange Morocco consciously and with some self-awareness presents itself as an "exotic" tourist destination. Another important source of income (and job creation) for Morocco is the spending by Western movie and television production companies. Morocco, in some ways, has encouraged and enabled this Western gaze. Because of its mountains, deserts, beaches, and architecturally fascinating cities, many directors have elected to produce their projects there. As early as 1962, five years after Morocco gained its independence, the iconic film *Lawrence of Arabia* was filmed there. More recent examples include *Black Hawk Down* (2001) based on a book about the U.S. military's raid on Mogadishu, *Captain Philips* (2013) starring Tom Hanks, based on the 2009 hijacking of the U.S. container ship Maersk Alabama by a crew of Somali pirates, and *American Sniper* (2014) starring Bradley Cooper about a Navy Seal who was a sniper in Iraq.

The issue of visiting a country like Morocco *without* viewing it through a colonial gaze is a complex but important one, mostly because of colonialism's lingering effects. I have tried my best throughout my travel life to engage in responsible and informed tourism, which sounds a bit high-minded, but I have come to believe it to be important.

Responsible and informed tourism requires educating oneself about a country's history, culture, and the effects of colonialism.

Responsible and informed tourism requires more listening and less talking.

Responsible and informed tourism requires being mindful in interactions with others, paying attention to the way we dress and interact with the people we meet, and being respectful of local customs.

Today, I do my best to encourage cultural humility. As an American, of course, there is a tendency to think that the American way of doing things is the best, wisest, and most ingenious. I have learned over and over, sometimes with embarrassment, that the American way of doing something may be *one way* of doing things, though not always the *best way*.

More than anything, I have always tried to remember that I am a guest in another's country.

15

'You Can't Go Home Again'

"You can't go back home to your family, back home to your childhood, back home to romantic love, back home to a young man's dreams of glory and of fame, back home to exile, to escape to Europe and some foreign land, back home to lyricism, to singing just for singing's sake, back home to aestheticism, to one's youthful idea of 'the artist' and the all-sufficiency of 'art' and 'beauty' and 'love,' back home to the ivory tower, back home to places in the country, to the cottage in Bermuda, away from all the strife and conflict of the world, back home to the father you have lost and have been looking for, back home to someone who can help you, save you, ease the burden for you, back home to the old forms and systems of things which once seemed everlasting but which are changing all the time—back home to the escapes of Time and Memory."

Thomas Wolfe, You Can't Go Home Again

I tried.

But, at the risk of spoiling this chapter's outcome: Thomas Wolfe was right in his astonishing 158-word sentence. And, of course, I've revealed as much myself in an earlier chapter, when I told you: "When I go to the Netherlands today, I cannot visit Grandma Minnie's Netherlands."

Yet, I was tempted—and I tried.

As many of my adventures do, this one started with coffee—in this case, coffee with a pastor who, like me, is retired. We were comparing notes about our lives. Even though he is Methodist and I am Presbyterian, we discovered that we had a great many experiences in common. In addition to our mutual membership in a lifelong learning academy, I discovered during our conversation that he also serves as a part-time pastor for a church near Holland, Michigan.

"It's very small," he said. "It's not a candidate for redevelopment. It probably won't be around in another ten years. There is only one traffic light in town, and the population in town is declining. But I feel as though I am doing some of the best pastoral work of my life."

I felt my eyes well up with tears. I knew immediately what he meant. He and I (and most pastors, presumably) want to do the best work that we are capable of doing. We take pride in preparing good sermons, for example. We want to provide leadership that is authentic and challenging. And even at, *especially* at, our ages, we want to be useful, still contributing and making a difference. I went home that afternoon and sent an email to my executive presbyter, which for Presbyterians is comparable to a bishop, and to her I wrote, "Put me to work."

She didn't, as it turned out, but not long after I received an email from someone else who invited me to go back to work. Not in a small town near Holland, Michigan, but in Europe, of all places. I would be returning to Europe in retirement to be a pastor in the Netherlands.

I found myself trying to go home, to what my grandmother described as the "old country." In fact, I found myself wishing that I could have told my grandmother about my plan. But, as I have already revealed in a previous chapter: When I go to the Netherlands today, I cannot visit Grandma Minnie's Netherlands.

In truth, I did not have much time to consider this journey. The fateful email came from an old friend who asked if I would become the interim pastor of a church in The Hague. This old friend was retiring in a few months, and a well-planned transition had hit an unexpected rough patch. Long story short, the church needed someone fast, someone with international church experience. My wife was not interested in going this time, but she could see that I wanted to go. As a compromise, we agreed that she would visit me for a few weeks in the fall and then again in the spring, and I agreed to come home for Christmas. So, I said yes to my old friend, and then I started the application for a residency permit. I turned in a considerable amount of paperwork (birth certificate, various diplomas, and much more), and I made plans to fly to Schiphol Airport in Amsterdam in mid-August, where two members of the church staff were going to welcome me and drive me to The Hague, the third largest city in the Netherlands and less than an hour's drive from Schiphol. I was told that there was an unusually large number of people seeking residency permits at the time, because of refugees from the war occurring then in Ukraine, so there might be a delay. But the permit was issued toward the end of the ninety-day window—in other words, right on time—and I went to work.

My commitment to the church in The Hague was for nine months or so—we were all a little vague about the end date—essentially the 2022-2023 school year. And unlike the church in Zürich, the church in The Hague owned a home, a three-story row house in a wonderful neighborhood, within easy walking or biking distance of the church. So, no need this time to search for an apartment. In fact, everything I needed—grocery store, hardware store, bakery, coffee shops, barber shop, even a fine restaurant (the Brasserie Le Quartier)—was within a short walk from my home.

I packed all the clothes and shoes I thought I would need into two large suitcases. I also decided to take my bike after first having it broken down and boxed at a bike shop for the flight. Taking a bike to the Netherlands seemed like an odd decision, as several people pointed out when I arrived. The population of the Netherlands is seventeen million, and there are an estimated twenty-four million bicycles. So, as I soon learned, bikes are not exactly a scarce commodity. I liked my own bike, though, mostly because of its large frame but also because, other than a few family photos, it was the only personal item I took with me.

Dutch people have a reputation for being direct, however, and one of my new Dutch friends said that "taking a bike to the Netherlands is like taking your own sand to the Middle East." It was not the last time I was to experience "Dutch directness," which is the opposite of the "Midwestern nice" of my childhood.

As for the rest of my packing, I made mostly good choices. I ended up buying two or three sweaters during the year to supplement my limited wardrobe, but otherwise I had everything I needed. What I could not have anticipated was how cold Dutch winters would be. I am from the upper Midwest, a cold-weather part of the U.S., but I discovered that there is something unexpectedly chilling about winters near the North Sea. I still don't understand why. Even though the canals haven't frozen over in several years, due to climate change, Dutch winters are unexpectedly cold.

That's what I wanted: to immerse myself in the life of the country where my family claimed to have roots and to learn more about everything—from the culture to the weather—than I had in several earlier visits to the Netherlands. I had visited briefly when I was seventeen; I had rented an apartment in August 2017 for a short stay to complete a book I was writing about multicultural churches. But I had wanted, and tried my best to welcome, this longer and deeper experience.

Although I have focused mainly on my grandmother, each of my grandparents came to the U.S. from the Netherlands. Beyond that, I grew up in a community with many Dutch immigrants. The church of my childhood was Dutch Reformed and once struggled with the decision to begin using English instead of Dutch in worship. I attended the college founded by that denomination, and most of the faculty at the time were the products of that same Dutch culture. And so, it's hardly surprising that I have always thought of myself as Dutch, even though no one I knew (except for my grandmother) spoke a word of Dutch. The truth is, despite the frequent claims to be Dutch, my community has been thoroughly assimilated into American culture. My mom told me not long ago that when Dad returned from military service in the Pacific following World War II, he said, "We are going to be Americans now." I suspect that something like that happened in many households following the war.

So, the big question for me—and you can transpose your own family's origins here—was: What did it mean for me to be Dutch? I thought I knew, but ethnic identity, as it turns out, is slippery. From that August day when I arrived in the Netherlands, my presumed identity as Dutch was challenged repeatedly. After getting off the overnight flight from the U.S., I approached a passport control agent who looked at my passport and said, in English, "You have a Dutch last name. Do you speak Dutch?"

"No," I said, "my grandparents immigrated to the U.S. but did not pass along the language."

With that answer, I could see his interest in me wane. He rattled off the next question: "How long will you be staying?"

I told him.

He stamped my passport. And he was on to the next new arrival.

That encounter at the airport turned out to be the first of many similar encounters—initial curiosity about my last name, followed by a rapid change of subject. I thought my last name somehow made me Dutch, but I was wrong.

Approximately one out of every five hundred people in the Netherlands shares my last name, but as far as I know I am not related to any of them. In August 1811, Napoleon issued a decree that everyone in what is now Belgium and the Netherlands was required to adopt a surname. And many people simply took their profession as that new surname—so, farmer (Boer), baker (Bakker), butcher (Slager), and fisher (Visser), to name a few. I seem to be descended from beer brewers, and nearly every modestly sized village had one of those, hence the number of people with my name. From my genealogical research, it appears that Rinze Davids Brouwer, at thirty-one years of age, was the first person in my family to take the name Brouwer, somewhere in the province of Groningen. Some Dutch people must have had a sense of humor at the time, too, because how else would you explain other names I found from that era: Naaktgeboren (born naked) and Pekelharing (pickled herring, a popular Dutch treat).

I arrived in the Netherlands thinking that on some level I finally was coming home. I thought my Dutch ancestry would be an advantage—that I would understand Dutch culture and that the people would understand me. I assumed, at the least, that I would be able to pronounce everyone's name correctly. I even remember thinking that "they will be very impressed." As it turned out, they weren't. Sometimes just the opposite.

Within a month of starting my new job, I went to a rehab center outside The Hague to visit a church member who was recovering from surgery. I went to the reception desk, as I would in the U.S., and said (using the Dutch words I had practiced and memorized), "I would like to see Trudy van der Meulen."

But the person at the front desk quickly sized me up as a native English speaker and said in English, "I don't think we have anyone with that last name."

"But I know she's here," I said, switching to English at her prompt.

"Oh," the person at the front desk said, "Did you mean Trudy van der Meulen?"

"That's what I said!"

"No, you didn't. But we do have a Trudy van der Meulen," she said, pronouncing the name, as far as I could tell, exactly the same way I had. And then she provided me with the room number and directions. I felt chastened but, more than that, I began to realize from my first weeks in the Netherlands that I was hardly as Dutch as I thought. I was an American—with some long-ago Dutch connections.

In the church I served as an interim pastor, there were many people who grew up with what might euphemistically be called "Dutch roots." Church members from Suriname, Indonesia, and South Africa grew up where the Dutch slave trade once flourished. In 1770 it is estimated that 5.2% of the overall Dutch economy was based on the Atlantic slave trade—and it was more than ten percent of the share in the wealthiest province in the Netherlands. The Dutch Reformed Church flourished in those places too, and it was the slave trade that brought Dutch people from Europe to live and work in those countries.

Over the last century, nearly all these former colonies (sometimes called "special municipalities") received their independence. Indonesia did not receive its independence from the Netherlands without a bloody four-year revolution, which occurred after the end of World War II. Suriname did not receive its independence until 1975, the year I graduated from my Dutch Reformed college. And the Dutch Caribbean (historically known as the Dutch West Indies) still includes some territories that are part of the Kingdom of the Netherlands.

Eventually, many people from these former or current colonies made their way to the Netherlands, found work, and stayed. Most were native Dutch speakers before they arrived.

The church I served, as it turned out, had many such members. They had different skin tones from the ones I associated with the Dutch—clearly different from my own—but they could claim a Dutch identity far more convincingly than I could. When I would listen to their stories, I realized that their claim to Dutch identity was in most ways stronger than my own, even though a hundred percent of my genetic inheritance can be traced to two provinces in the northern part of the country. When I was with them, in fact, I would often feel like a pretender, someone who enjoyed calling himself "Dutch," when everyone could plainly see and hear that I was not.

Three months into my stay, I began to have feelings common to many expats. It was Thanksgiving Day—what the Dutch call "just another Thursday"—and I had mostly recovered from a relatively mild case of COVID-19. It's never good to be sick so far from home. I was walking in the early morning darkness to the Den Haag Centraal Station where I planned to catch a train to Leiden for an American Thanksgiving service, and suddenly a wave of loneliness and homesickness came over me. I was in a strange country—still strange in most ways, even after three months, even with the loveliest of people to work with—and I was missing what was an important holiday to me. My family was in the U.S., and I was not. I was on the wrong side of the Atlantic—on my way to work—with no dinner plans and no football game to watch.

"What am I doing here?" I nearly said aloud.

What kept me going was that I wanted to meet the new U.S. ambassador to the Netherlands, as well as the other clergy who were participating in the service, including the rabbi at the Liberal Jewish Congregation of The Hague, who was assigned to sit next to me in the front row. (We entertained each other by telling jokes and offering commentary on the service as it went along.) Ordinarily, I thrive on making new friends and having new experiences, but on this particular day I wanted to be somewhere else.

Beyond the feelings of sadness and homesickness, I had also been apprehensive about the interfaith service. My previous experience with American expats wasn't always positive and that to a degree shaped my expectations about the service. The American expats I met in Switzerland often kept to themselves. They frequently lived in a certain neighborhood near Zürich, they sent their children to the American school, and they didn't learn the local language or try very hard to mingle with their Swiss neighbors. 'Aloof' was the vibe that many experienced from those Americans. This is a generalization, but it was my experience. And because of it, I imagined that the Thanksgiving service I was heading to would be a kind of rally for lonely, aloof Americans. I half-expected to hear the chant "USA, USA!"

The Pieterskerk, where the service was being held, turned out to be a gorgeous old church in Leiden's old city. It was built around 1100, and for a few hundred years, it was a Catholic church. Then, in the sixteenth century, it became a Protestant church. And in 1975 it ceased being a church altogether and became instead an event center. This story—Catholic to Protestant to secular meeting space—describes many of the old churches in the Netherlands. If there is any good news in this, the church buildings are being well maintained and they remain in use, sometimes even for Christian worship.

By the end of the service, I felt pretty good about having gone. The music was beautiful, an important story was told, and—as the mayor of Leiden put it in his remarks to several hundred Americans in attendance—it was as though we had gathered in the living room of a dear friend and had a good conversation. The church, I should mention, has a memorial to the pilgrims who are credited with starting the Thanksgiving tradition in North America. The story, which I knew only in vague terms, is that English Protestants, who later came to be known as "pilgrims," fled England to escape the oppressive regime of James I and the Anglican Church. They lived and worked in Leiden from 1609 to 1620 and worshipped at the Pieterskerk, before many, though not all, of them continued their journey to the "new world." The mayor told this story with such sweetness and humor that for me it very nearly redeemed the day.

For much of my life, I have listened to U.S. politicians talk about the "socialist nightmare" in Western Europe—the heavy tax burden, inefficient welfare systems, bureaucracy that stifles imagination and entrepreneurship. In other words, the opposite of everything that the U.S. aspires to represent to the world. But while living in the Netherlands, I experienced something quite different, something I also experienced for the five years I lived in Switzerland. My experience, I must say, was quite pleasant, far from a nightmare. The people I met—my neighbors, the shopkeepers in my neighborhood, the church members I came to know—are generally happy.

Maybe they are unaware that they are living in a dystopia, with great suffering and injustice, though I doubt it. The Dutch people I met can be quite critical of their government. They regularly complain and point out government stupidity. When then-prime minister, Mark Rutte, apologized during my time in the country for the Dutch role in the slave trade, I remember that one of my church members responded angrily and wondered why anyone needed to apologize for what was done hundreds of years ago. The Dutch king, Willem-Alexander, offered a similar apology seven months later.

But here's the thing: The Dutch are not eager to live anywhere else, certainly not in the U.S. Some of them travel to the U.S., but mostly they are quite happy where they are. The Netherlands (in contrast to the U.S.) consistently ranks as one of the world's happiest countries. Other northern European countries do as well. The U.S. ranked fifteenth in 2023, up one place from 2022, but not exactly the happiest place on Earth. Nearly everyone I met, in fact, looked across the ocean at the U.S. with disbelief. They would shake their heads, for example, over the gun culture and the mass shootings in the U.S. They would ask me how the country with the world's largest economy and military could be struggling so visibly. Far from jealousy, what I sensed was alarm. For my part, I was alarmed by the relatively high tax rate I had to pay while in the Netherlands.

Then, I looked around and noticed that the roads and infrastructure were quite good, better than much of what I see in the U.S., certainly better than in Michigan, where I now live. When I lived in the Netherlands, my work sometimes took me to The Hague's poorer neighborhoods, but I never saw anything that compares to the suffering and squalor in several places in my own country, which proudly calls itself "the richest country in the world." There is poverty in the Netherlands, but the social safety net works—mostly—and takes care of what the Bible calls "the least of these." People in the Netherlands often repeated what I heard more than once in Switzerland—namely, "we as a country are more Christian than you are." It was not an easy indictment to hear. They are proud of their system. It's not perfect, but it works for them.

The Netherlands is not a very religious country. It once was, of course, as all of Europe was, and visiting old churches, which today are more museum than church, was my favorite activity on my day off. But the rates of religious affiliation have fallen to low levels in the Netherlands, as they have throughout much of Europe. Even with that, though, there are some surprisingly vibrant Christian communities in Europe, and I was able to serve two of them during my career.

So, why don't I just move there if I like it so much?

One answer is that I finally learned the Netherlands is not my home and I am more American than Dutch.

But there is something more. Something unexpected happened to me in my nine months abroad: I knew where I wanted to be. Always for me the inner longing has been for home, but home—the place where I wanted to be—was western Michigan. I grew up there. My community shaped me in profound ways, often in good ways, though not always. Along the way I have rejected a great deal, but I have also retained a great deal. I am the person I am today because I grew up in western Michigan, near a lake that I would visit every summer, even when I lived hundreds—sometimes thousands—of miles away.

In what sense is western Michigan my home? Even now I can't explain that precisely. What I know is that I feel it when I'm there. It is familiar to me in a way that dozens of other places never were.

As we come toward the end of this journey together, I wonder how you might answer those questions:

Where is home for you?

What makes it home?

16

How Can We Write the Final Chapter?

"The things that began to happen after that were so great and beautiful that I cannot write them. And for us, this is the end of all the stories."
C.S. Lewis, *The Last Battle*

John couldn't do it.

He ends his Gospel with the admission: "But there are also many other things that Jesus did; if every one of them were written down, I suppose that the world itself could not contain the books that would be written." I can picture him sighing wearily. There is still so much more to write! And yet, after what we know today as Chapter 21, he laid down his pen (if that's what he used to write) and his Gospel was finished.

C.S. Lewis couldn't do it in Narnia. The long final sentence of *The Chronicles of Narnia* includes his admission that he could not find words to describe what comes next for his characters. He affirms that "they were beginning Chapter One of the Great Story that no one on Earth has read"—and that's how he closes his seven-novel cycle, without even attempting to summarize the rest of that journey.

J.R.R. Tolkien gave up, as well. On the final page of *The Lord of the Rings*, the ailing Frodo is sailing off toward the Havens and "smelled a sweet fragrance on the air and heard the sound of singing that came over the water." Frodo and friends pass through a curtain, glimpse "a swift sunrise"—and … and, that's all. The great *Rings* saga is over.

So, who am I to write about the final journey?

What I can share with you is some of my own restless grappling with images, metaphors, and some of the guides who have prompted my own yearnings about the last adventure. I also can urge you to start sorting through your own collection of family, community, cultural, and spiritual stories about this final journey. None of us like to talk about the end, but death comes for all of us.

So, please, before you go, let's talk about this one last adventure.

To bucket or not to bucket

Let's start with something one step removed from the end, something Americans love to talk about these days, something that has sparked an entirely fresh wave of tourism: bucket lists.

The origin of the term "bucket list" is obscure, but the 2007 film called *The Bucket List*, starring Morgan Freeman and Jack Nicholson, cemented the term in the modern consciousness. Having found widespread use, the term even entered the Oxford English Dictionary, though not until 2013. Today just about everyone knows that a bucket list is a list of experiences or achievements people hope to complete before they die—or "kick the bucket" (an English idiom which also has an obscure origin).

Former President Barack Obama once staged an impromptu visit to Stonehenge in 2014 following a NATO summit in Wales and announced to a curious press corps that, with his visit to the site, he had "knocked it off the bucket list." Presumably, "become president of the United States" ranked higher than "see Stonehenge," but Obama's complete list has never been made public. In photographs I've seen, Obama seemed genuinely excited to be there, but dropping by Stonehenge for ten minutes and then announcing that you've crossed it off your bucket list suggests that seeing Stonehenge—or standing in front of the Taj Mahal, or visiting the Louvre, or observing a pride of lions under a tree in the Maasai Mara Reserve in Kenya—is "something that, having been done, can be considered done with," as Rebecca Mead memorably put it in a *New Yorker* essay around that time.

In the film version of *The Bucket List*, the main characters meet in a hospital room because they have both been diagnosed with a terminal form of cancer. Together they decide that before they die, they must go places and see things. And so, improbably, the two geriatric cancer patients set off to see the Pyramids, the Taj Mahal, Hong Kong, the French Riviera, and the Himalayas—an impressive list, I must say, even for two younger, healthier people.

The late film critic Roger Ebert panned the film and described the travel experiences portrayed in the film as "an orgy of male bonding." In his words, "*The Bucket List* thinks dying of cancer is a laff [sic] riot followed by a dime-store epiphany." He imagined that most cancer patients lying in their hospital beds would not recognize themselves if they happened to see the film. However, the general public received the film more charitably, and it grossed more than $175 million.

The film may have advanced the idea that bucket lists are primarily about *places* we want to see before we die, but the truth—I am happy to report—is that bucket lists can be quite varied and often surprising. Not everyone, as it turns out, wants to go somewhere and see something and then be done with it. The website bucketlist.net is a kind of exchange where people write a bucket list and then invite others to give them advice or help them accomplish an item on the list. "Forty-one years old and never been kissed" was a predictable entry, I suppose. But I thought, "Are you a pianist who could give me a lesson; I would at least like to play 'A River Flows In You' before I die" was touching.

Overall, I'm leaning more toward Ebert's skepticism. The general approach to bucket lists as a "check off the boxes" approach to life seems shallow to me—and often self-centered, if not downright selfish. Since we're talking about films, consider instead the 1946 classic *It's a Wonderful Life*. George Bailey, the main character who is played by Jimmy Stewart, never achieved anything on his bucket list—like going to college, becoming an architect, and escaping the narrow confines of Bedford Falls. But, when given a miraculous opportunity to reflect on his life, George concludes that he has lived a worthwhile life after all. In fact, his commitment to self-sacrifice over many years made a difference in more lives than he was aware. And that's one reason people still cherish the film nearly eighty years later. I think, like George, we all have a sneaking suspicion that checking items off a bucket list does not always lead to happiness.

So, why *do* people compile bucket lists? What *function* do they serve?

As it turns out, these and many similar questions have been thoroughly studied and examined. Interestingly, one important reason people compile bucket lists is less about living life fully and more about the fear of dying. Something called Terror Management Theory, which arose in the '70s and '80s, and is now known as TMT, is often cited in this connection. People seek meaning in life, according to this theory, in part to manage insecurities related to the awareness of their death. In other words, by perceiving their lives as meaningful, people push back on their existential worries. Bucket lists, in this view, are a kind of negotiation with life expectancy. The lists signify—at least to the person who compiles the list—a life well lived.

Arthur C. Brooks, who teaches at both the Kennedy School of Government at Harvard and the Harvard Business School, has acknowledged in a fine *Atlantic Monthly* essay titled "How to Want Less" that novelty can sometimes be fun and even exciting. New and unexpected experiences activate the brain's reward pathway more powerfully than familiar ones, leading to a greater dopamine release and a more intense sense of pleasure. American Heart Association research has even demonstrated how pre-trip planning brings happiness, and taking vacation time has been linked to more positive cardiovascular health outcomes.

But here's the caveat: On its own, excitement won't bring about *enduring* happiness. Human beings, as Brooks puts it, "habituate rapidly to what is new." Bucket lists are essentially a list of dreams, and Brooks writes that "dreams are liars." When dreams come true, we are happy, but only for a short time. Then a new dream appears and, in his words, "our idea of equilibrium is reset." And this is his rather blunt conclusion: "When we build a life centered on achievement, we are focused on the wrong side of the happiness equation. We are cultivating a list of hopeful haves instead of reducing our list of wants."

Kate Bowler, a professor of history at Duke University Divinity School, was thirty-five years old when her doctors told her that she had stage IV colon cancer and, in her words, "a slim chance of survival." Her diagnosis triggered a series of mental health assessments at the cancer clinic where she was treated, and "the lovely and well-meaning counselors, all seemingly named Caitlin" told her that she should consider making a bucket list. Other patients, she was told, found the exercise to be "clarifying."

Happily, after years of being told she was incurable, she was declared cancer free. During her treatments, she wrote two *New York Times* bestselling memoirs, including *No Cure For Being Human (and Other Truths I Need to Hear)*. In that book, she includes an entire chapter on bucket lists. The "Caitlins" at the cancer clinic, she writes, were surprisingly persistent, even providing helpful prompts: "What new skill could I learn?" they wondered. "What classic movies should I watch? Is there a passion I might reignite? Cross-stitching? Restoring a vintage car? Soaring in a hot-air balloon?"

As a historian who specializes in the history of Christianity, Bowler was aware that, with the ascendance of Christianity under Emperor Constantine in the fourth century, a different form of bucket list emerged—namely, the pilgrimages that we explored earlier in this book. Churches and shrines were built over places made sacred by Jesus and the apostles, and Christians made it a point to visit those churches and shrines, sometimes walking long distances to get there. And so began, she writes, "a holy travel circuit that believers have been making ever since."

Bowler doesn't have much to say—good or bad—about ancient pilgrimages, though one senses that she is not a huge fan. Instead, she reserves her choicest words for what came after the pilgrimage, which she describes as the "modern bucket list." I like the way she puts it: "There are enough activities in the modern bucket list industry to keep people industriously morbid. It is a form of experiential capitalism. Hang gliding. Snorkeling. Times Square on New Year's Eve and Paris in the spring." Bowler even wrote an opinion column for *The New York Times* in 2021 titled, "One Thing I Don't Plan to Do Before I Die Is Make a Bucket List."

I have not made a bucket list either and don't plan to do so. Or perhaps I should clarify that I have not written or typed anything resembling a list. I do think about places I would like to visit and things I would like to see. I have done this for much of my life. As I finished editing this book, in fact, I left home for weeks of walking the Portuguese Camino, which like the Camino Frances I walked in 2019, ends in Santiago de Compostela in northwestern Spain. Having written about my frightening experience on my first Camino, and finally admitting to myself that I have a few limitations, I am planning to work with a travel company this time and plan where I will stop each night.

I have discussed other travel adventures with my wife, who has indicated that she has "seen enough" of Europe and no longer feels a need to go there. As a result, we have been dreaming a little of New Zealand or Australia. One of my seminary classmates spent his entire career on the island of Tasmania, south of Australia, and I would love to travel there and say hello and see his unique ministry setting. Another friend from my years in Zürich, Switzerland, has returned to his native Sydney, Australia. He has indicated that he would like to show me around. Still another friend from my days in Switzerland has returned to Melbourne, Australia, where she teaches at the university there. I would love to see her again too.

Does *Sehnsucht* call us backward or onward?

In short, I've never lost my *Sehnsucht*. That's the German word I mentioned at the outset of our journey together through these pages. It's a hard-to-define German term—a yearning for something that might somehow complete us. Yearning. Longing. A bittersweet blend of desire and melancholy. The feeling is at once beautiful and painful.

For many Americans, this yearning is for the past—a nostalgia for an America that may have existed briefly in the 1950s, but if it did it exist then, it existed only in certain suburbs and certainly not for everyone. I vaguely remember it, but I've never been quite sure if it was real. For others, there is a kind of grieving that we will never experience such a time and place again.

For me, the yearning is not for the past, and certainly not for the American suburbs of the 1950s. Surprisingly, my yearning is not for the U.S. at all. To be back briefly after months away was to recognize the good and the bad of American life. I was overwhelmed at times by the friendliness and helpfulness of people in Holland, Michigan, where I vacationed each summer and where I planned to retire. I recognized myself in those people. I was even aware, as I am today, that I look like them—and they like me. But I was also irritated by them—their dependence on automobiles, their wastefulness, their loudness, all the ways they were like me.

My friends in Switzerland, who were also far from home, would often refer to their "passport country"—meaning, I sensed, that their *citizenship* was somewhere else, but their home was here, with me, with their church, and with their friends. Still, there was always, for all of us, the sense that we did not belong here either, not even in Switzerland, not really.

Sehnsucht is a recurring theme in German literature, from Goethe's *Faust* to Rilke's *Duino Elegies*. It has also inspired musicians, such as Schubert and Schumann. But no one tried harder, it seems to me, than C.S. Lewis (hardly a German) to wrestle a new depth of meaning from the word. Lewis, as I mentioned, described *Sehnsucht* as the "inconsolable longing" in the human heart for "we know not what." I see this theme, as a matter of fact, in much of his writing, especially in the *Chronicles of Narnia*. I think I see it in much of my life—which might begin to account for my seemingly insatiable desire to see and experience so much of the world, to keep my passport in my back pocket, just in case.

I know of course that this inconsolable longing, this *Sehnsucht*, is, more than anything, spiritual. If more than forty years of being a pastor teaches you anything at all, it teaches you to see spiritual connections everywhere. I once read Augustine when I was a Princeton Seminary student, but in your early twenties you know so little about life. The young man I was then, I'm afraid, knew even less than most. "You have made us for yourself," I remember reading in the opening sentences of Augustine's great autobiographical work *Confessions*. "And our hearts are restless, until they find rest in you." Now—at long last—those words are beginning to make sense to me. My heart has always been restless. And I now see that what I have known is a *spiritual* restlessness—not an adventure gene, except maybe in a small way, but primarily a longing for a spiritual home, *my* home. Restlessness like this, I have come to see, is not a flaw, not a sign of that there is something wrong with me, but a sign of God's presence in my life. A person of faith might even say that it is a divinely planted yearning for God.

After all my bravado in the first chapter about loading everything I owned into a car and setting out into the world at age twenty—determined to succeed or die trying—I feel compelled to mention that, after more than forty years of being away, thousands of miles away at the end, I did eventually move back. My wife and I made western Michigan our home in retirement. We had talked about it often, discussed it at length, but the reality always seemed to be far in the future. But the day finally came, and when it did, we moved back. In hindsight, the decision always had a kind of inevitability about it. We built a home in the beach association where our family vacationed every summer. We can now walk to the beach any time we want and see those sunsets that I was once able to see only in my mind's eye. We can go for long walks on the beach any day of the week—in fact, any time of the year.

So, here I am at last, a place I couldn't wait to leave. Whether I returned home a success or not, I don't know. I feel successful in some ways, but not in others. I suppose my ideas of success have changed over the years—along with much else. When I returned, I was not the same person who left, and the place I had left behind—to my surprise—had changed as well. I recognized some things, of course, but much that I saw was new, had been updated, or had simply disappeared.

After I left western Michigan, I lived in six states—New Jersey, Iowa, Pennsylvania, Illinois, Michigan (the eastern side, which should be a different state), and Florida. And as if that were not enough moving around, toward the end my career I lived and worked in Switzerland and the Netherlands. I was married in my mid-twenties—to the girlfriend who insisted on sending that houseplant along with me to Princeton, New Jersey—and we lived for the first fifteen months of our marriage in Iowa City, Iowa, the only time I have ever lived west of the Mississippi River.

Our first daughter was born in Pennsylvania, the second one in New Jersey. I returned to Princeton Seminary at one point for an additional academic degree, as though my first one was not enough, and then I served a church a few miles from the seminary campus for five years. I twice lived in university towns, once in a state capitol, once in the suburb of a large city, and once in Fort Lauderdale. The longest I lived anywhere was for thirteen years—Wheaton, Illinois, in the western suburbs of Chicago—and that sojourn now seems like an extraordinarily long time.

I have led study tours, made pilgrimages, and gone on mission trips to every continent except Antarctica. I don't know for sure, but I suspect that I have set out more than most people. And along the way, I have not only been challenged, but have been shaped and molded by each new experience. I am not the same person I was at twenty. My hair is gray, for one thing, and I have lost an inch in height. Curiously, I no longer sound like the Midwesterner I once was, thanks to the seminary speech professor who cringed when he first heard me speak. But am I wiser? I hope so, though I wonder about that, along with much else.

I know that other people have moved around and have had many more experiences than I have had. I have met *many* people, in fact, who fit this description. When I served that church in Zürich, Switzerland, I was pastor to people who had moved far greater distances and had to adapt to far more diverse cultures. A family from India, to give one example, had lived for several years in Saudi Arabia before their move to Europe. The cultural changes they have experienced far exceed anything I have experienced, and their story, I discovered, was far from the exception. Still, I moved a lot—at least that's the way it has felt to me. And each time I moved, I was excited to be somewhere new, always curious, always wondering if I would be up to the challenge.

Inward or outward?

So, this brings me to yet another of these final questions, which we might pose as: backward or onward?

In other words: Does *Sehnsucht* call us inward or outward?

These days, Joseph Campbell's work is both studied and criticized. His sexism throughout his career has led a generation of scholars to point out all the women in the world's cultural heritage whom he ignored or dismissed in his work. But in speaking with groups around the country, I still hear people asking about his signature "hero's journey." From one perspective, much of Campbell's description might be applied to my life, even returning home at the end of my adventures. My own criticism of Campbell's hero's journey framework is that it lacks a spiritual component. I suppose some might argue that the journey to self-discovery is itself a spiritual task, but with my theological training, I wonder if the hero, as Campbell imagines him, needs much divine help. On the other hand, the spiritual component can be easily adapted to Campbell's framework. The hero, as Campbell imagines him, could easily have a spiritual awakening or experience a divine calling. The hero could face challenges that test the hero's faith or beliefs. The hero might even make a pilgrimage to a sacred place—or participate in a ritual or ceremony that marks the hero's spiritual transformation. I have experienced all—or at least most—of that.

What concerns me about his hero's journey, though, is its largely inner direction—as though the journey is always about oneself. "Being a blessing"—what I remember from childhood about the call of Abraham to set out "to the land I will show you"—seems to be mostly absent from Campbell's framework. Once again, it is easy enough to adapt this "other directed" focus, but Campbell does not emphasize what has been for me a critically important dimension of my life, my work, and my many adventures. I would like to think that my life, like Abraham's, has been a blessing.

Perhaps other writers might spark more contemporary and spirited discussions with friends about the adventures we have experienced—through my writing and your own reflections on memories we have sparked in these pages. Consider Hunter S. Thompson, for example. One of my favorite Thompson quotes goes like this: "Life should not be a journey to the grave with the intention of arriving safely in a pretty and well-preserved body, but rather to skid in broadside in a cloud of smoke, thoroughly used up, totally worn out, and loudly proclaiming, 'Wow! What a ride!'"

Thompson himself certainly seemed to live that way. His life—what I know about it—seemed like a wild ride. But I never really wanted that for myself, and I'm not sure why I like the quote so much, except that it was one person's startlingly honest declaration. It's not clear to me that Thompson's life led to anything close to self-awareness, let alone being a blessing to others. Maybe Thompson did come to the end of his life with a richer, fuller understanding of himself. And maybe he did bless a few people along the way. I hope so. He sometimes blessed me with his writing. What I have read, though, suggests that alcohol and drugs filled Thompson's last months and that he took his own life at the age of sixty-seven.

For me, searching, discovering, exploring, meeting people from around the world—that was what I wanted, that was what I needed, and so that was what I pursued. Instead of feeling "thoroughly used up, totally worn out," I find myself feeling grateful for what I have been able to do, sometimes overwhelmed with how rich my life has been. And I am not finished. My wife and I just renewed our passports, and I can see in mine many blank pages ready for new stamps.

'One more surprise'

In the mid-1990s, I became aware of a song—"I Was There To Hear Your Borning Cry"—that had been written ten years earlier by John Ylvisaker, a Lutheran composer from Minnesota who died in 2017. We tried it at my Wheaton church as a song for the congregation to sing after a baptism, and it caught on. Families began to request it. In the years since, I have read complaints that the song hardly ranks up there with those richly textured (and theologically rich) hymns from centuries earlier, but the song, I think, works just fine on its own. In important ways, it is better and more accessible. And its theological message always seems just right for those who sing it.

> *I was there to hear your borning cry,*
> *I'll be there when you are old.*
> *I rejoiced the day you were baptized,*
> *to see your life unfold.*
> *I was there when you were but a child,*
> *with a faith to suit you well;*
> *In a blaze of light you wandered off*
> *to find where demons dwell.*
>
> *When you heard the wonder of the Word*
> *I was there to cheer you on;*
> *You were raised to praise the living Lord,*
> *to whom you now belong.*
> *If you find someone to share your time*
> *and you join your hearts as one,*
> *I'll be there to make your verses rhyme*
> *from dusk 'till rising sun.*

In the middle ages of your life,
not too old, no longer young,
I'll be there to guide you through the night,
complete what I've begun.
When the evening gently closes in,
and you shut your weary eyes,
I'll be there as I have always been
with just one more surprise.

I was there to hear your borning cry,
I'll be there when you are old.
I rejoiced the day you were baptized,
to see your life unfold.

Several lines in the song always struck me. One was "in a blaze of light you wandered off to see where demons dwell." That might describe other people I have known, but I never thought it described my life. I don't think I "wandered off," because I always felt purposeful in my traveling. "Demons?" No. I found some, of course. I suppose everyone does. But that was never what compelled me.

It was another line that has always intrigued me. "When the evening gently closes in, and you shut your weary eyes, I'll be there as I have always been with just one more surprise." That phrase "one more surprise" became my way of thinking about death—and, in particular, my own death. With that language, death suddenly became for me one more adventure, one more *worthy* adventure to look forward to. Death, instead of something to be feared or avoided, could be something to get ready for, to anticipate, as I have for so many of the adventures of my life.

I don't know what comes next.

My ninety-six-year-old Mom seemed to have a clear idea. In the last weeks of her life, she said she wanted to see "Jack" again. "Jack" was my dad, and in Mom's imagination they will be together again, which to me sounds like a strong endorsement of their nearly seventy years together. She also hopes to see her father again. He died a year before I was born, and she has missed him ever since. I have heard enough about him that I would like to introduce myself and hear stories about his life.

But I am not as sure as Mom about what lies ahead. I suspect that something does. I have never been one of those who says, "When you're gone, you're gone." That could turn out to be true, of course, but my faith tells me there's more—more to see and taste and experience.

And whatever it is, I want to be there.

My passport is ready, with lots of blank pages. I sold my fancy Nikon camera and stopped taking photos a few years ago, but I still have a good eye for perspective and interesting angles. I still have a well-developed sense of wonder. I still cry when I see something beautiful.

And so, that's what I look forward to.

One more surprise.

Acknowledgments

Only in recent years, as I look back over my life, has it become clear to me that my curiosity—my near-constant need to go places and see things—was a gift from Mom and Dad. There were those summer road trips, which I describe in chapter two, but there was much more. Like all children, I assumed that my childhood experience was widely shared, but that turned out not to be the case. Simply put, I had curious parents, far more curious than most, and their curiosity nudged me toward a life of adventure. For that I will always be grateful.

I had two sets of grandparents who loved me unconditionally, but it was my Grandma Minnie (born Jacomina Glerum in the Netherlands) who introduced me to what she called the "old country." Her Vermeer wall prints, Delft tea sets, and Dutch liqueurs (always around the holidays) suggested to a young grandson that the world was far bigger and far more interesting than the world I knew in western Michigan. I wish I could have told her about that time I lived in The Hague for nine months and tried my best to learn her native language. She would have loved hearing about it.

A conversation over dinner one night with my younger daughter at a restaurant in The Hague, of all places, led to choosing the subject for this book. My older daughter is no less an adventurer than my younger daughter, which is how I feel whenever I sit in

How Can We Write the Final Chapter? 193

her congregation and listen to her preach. Both daughters, in different ways, inspired this book.

Over the years I have participated in several writers' groups made up of like-minded people with whom I have shared book chapters, stories, and even poems—and in which I read and commented on the writing of others. The longest continuing group is a small one; it includes only Pat Locke and me. The two of us go back almost thirty years. For her generous support and patient reading, which now includes this book, I am more grateful than I can express. For this book I am indebted to a group that includes Jeff Munroe, Rhonda Edgington, Laurie Baron, Lynn Jappinga, and Mark Hiskes. Their comments and suggestions made the book much stronger than it would have been, and I am deeply grateful.

And then there are the people who have read chapters of this book, offered generous encouragement, and even seemed to suggest (if I heard them correctly) that I might have a book worth reading: Arjan Overwater, Olinka Kazar, Marvin Hage, M.D., and Jack Dils. Jack was someone I met on my first solo pilgrimage (across northern Spain in 2019), and it made sense to ask him what he thought of my reflections.

The churches where my passion for mission and pilgrimage was most strongly encouraged were the First Presbyterian Church of Wheaton, Illinois, and the First Presbyterian Church of Ann Arbor, Michigan. I am deeply indebted to members of both churches. And I am especially indebted to the youth of the Wheaton church for overlooking my complete lack of youth ministry skills and spending time with me anyway. I will always fondly remember those summer mission trips.

Not many pastors get to serve international congregations, and I have been able to serve three. I served the International Protestant Church in Zürich, Switzerland, as pastor for several years and got to experience life in a beautiful European city. Then, not quite finished with my life's vocation, I returned twice to Europe and served two congregations as interim pastor—one in Lucerne, Switzerland, and the other in The Hague, in the Netherlands. In all three churches I met people from all over the world and will always be grateful for what they taught me about their history and culture. I hope I represented my own history and culture with humility and authenticity.

I am deeply grateful to David Crumm and Susan Stitt, both of Front Edge Publishing. David spent hours with me before publication, often reviewing my manuscript line by line, as we attempted to make this book as good as it could be. I have worked with some fine editors over the years, but this effort on my behalf was extraordinary.

And then there is my most frequent travel partner and most enthusiastic supporter. My wife Susan has gone along with me on my adventures, but just as often she has driven me to the airport and waved goodbye and then waited patiently at home for me to return. I could not have lived this life of adventure and travel, of going places and seeing things, without her support and love.

About the Author

Beginning with family road trips as a child, Douglas J. Brouwer has traveled throughout his life—and has written, spoken and taught about the transformative power of travel. He has led mission trips, pilgrimages, and study tours to countries around the world—and in recent years he has discovered the joys and challenges of walking solo along the various Camino paths in Spain and Portugal.

Doug has been a Presbyterian pastor for forty-five years, serving churches in the U.S. and Europe, including Wheaton, Illinois, Ann Arbor, Michigan, and Fort Lauderdale, Florida. Before his retirement, he served for five years as pastor of an international congregation in Zürich, Switzerland. He also has returned twice to Europe to serve as an interim pastor, once in Lucerne, Switzerland, and most recently in The Hague, The Netherlands. His previous books include *Chasing After Wind: A Pastor's Life*, *Remembering the Faith: What Christians Believe*, and *How to Become A Multicultural Church*. He is a frequent contributor to publications such as ReformedJournal.com and Englewood Review of Books.

Doug received his undergraduate degree from Calvin University (formerly Calvin College) and his Master of Divinity and Doctor of Ministry degrees from Princeton Theological Seminary.

His wife and frequent travel partner, Susan DeYoung, was an attorney in private practice for most of her career. She retired as executive director of Habitat for Humanity in Broward County, Florida. Their older daughter is a Presbyterian pastor in St. Paul, Minnesota, and their younger daughter is a health economist who lives in Seattle, Washington.

Connect With Douglas J. Brouwer

Thank you for reading *The Traveler's Path*. If you enjoyed this book, and think that others would find it helpful, please leave a review on Amazon or Goodreads.com.

A discussion guide is available for download at reformedjournal.com/books.

If you'd like more information about Douglas J. Brouwer or about *The Traveler's Path*, please visit and subscribe to Doug's blog: DougsBlog.substack.com.

If you'd like to have Douglas Brouwer speak to your church, community group, or be a guest on your podcast, he is available to do so. Contact Douglas J. Brouwer at douglas.brouwer@gmail.com.

You can also connect with Doug on these social media sites:
Amazon.com/stores/author/B001KIV7RG/about
Goodreads.com/author/show/429385.Douglas_J_Brouwer
Facebook.com/douglas.brouwer.1
Instagram.com/douglasbrouwer
LinkedIn.com/in/douglasbrouwer
Threads.net/@douglasbrouwer
Bsky.app/profile/douglasbrouwer.bsky.social

TELLING STORIES IN THE DARK
by Jeffrey Munroe

Millions live with sorrow, trauma, and grief. Jeffrey Munroe and a national array of experts explore true stories of resiliency, hope, and faith as people transform pain and find fresh inspiration.

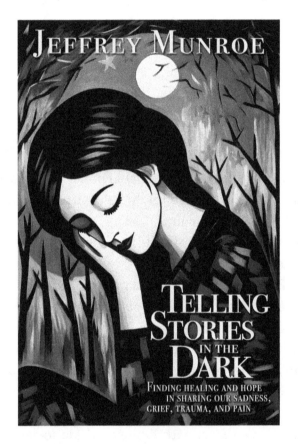

Reformed Journal Books

https://reformedjournal.com/all-books

New in 2025!

GREEN STREET IN BLACK AND WHITE
A Chicago Story
by
Dave Larsen

In the early 1960s on Green Street, a boy and his friends face challenges in a neighborhood brimming with racial change. Dave Larsen takes us back to a summer of social upheaval, when youthful mischief collided with the weight of adult fears.

Reformed Journal Books

https://reformedjournal.com/all-books/

www.ingramcontent.com/pod-product-compliance
Lightning Source LLC
Chambersburg PA
CBHW030412070325
22922CB00005B/15